Cost and Finance of Higher Education in Mizoram

About the Author

Abdul Hannan Barbhuiya is presently working as an Assistant Professor and Head in the Department of Economics, Kamalanagar College, Chawngte, Mizoram. He completed his MA (Economics) from the North Eastern Hill University, Shillong, in 1999 and LLB from Mizoram University, Aizawl, in 2005. After completing his M.Phil (Economics) from Madurai Kamaraj University, Madurai, T.N. in 2008, he obtained his Doctoral Degree in Economics from the Mizoram University, Aizawl in 2011.

Dr. Barbhuiya is actively engaged in teaching and research works. He has participated and contributed a number of research papers in various international, national, regional and state level seminars, workshops and conferences. He is a life member of the North Eastern Economic Association (NEEA) and Mizoram Economic Association (MEA).

Cost and Finance of Higher Education in Mizoram

Abdul Hannan Barbhuiya

CONCEPT PUBLISHING COMPANY PVT. LTD.,
NEW DELHI-110059

(A publication subsidy of Rs. 20,000 only was sanctioned by N.C.E.R.T., New Delhi, facilitated the publication of this book. The author acknowledges it with due gratitude).

ISPN-13: 978-93-5125-039-5

First Published 2014

Published and Printed by

Concept
Since 1974

Concept Publishing Company Pvt. Ltd.
A/15-16, Commercial Block, Mohan Garden
New Delhi-110059 (India)
T: 25351460, 25351794, *F*: 091-11-25357109
E: publishing@conceptpub.com, W: www.conceptpub.com
Editorial Office: H-13, Bali Nagar, New Delhi-110 015, India.

Cataloging in Publication Data--Courtesy: D.K. Agencies (P) Ltd. <docinfo@dkagencies.com>

Barbhuiya, Abdul Hannan.
Cost and finance of higher education in Mizoram / Abdul Hannan Barbhuiya.
p. cm.
Includes bibliographical references (p.) and index.
ISBN 9789351250395

1. Education, Higher—India—Mizoram—Finance. 2. Higher education and state India—Mizoram. I. Title.

DDC 379.12140954166 23

Foreword

It is my pleasure to write the foreword of a book viz., "Cost and Finance of Higher Education in Mizoram" by Dr. Abdul Hannan Barbhuiya. The subject 'cost of education' is not only important but also contemporary. It is especially relevant for Mizoram which happens to be the third highest literate state in India. In the absence of adequate physical resources, the only option is to depend on human resources for economic development through a planned development of education.

Important areas of research in this field may broadly be identified as contribution of education to economic growth and financial aspects of educational systems. The present book is an authentic work by the author on the cost and finance of higher education in the state of Mizoram. It is based on extensive field study and empirical research, which will provide first-hand information to the readers. The first two chapters of the book deal with the introduction of the study and the geographical and administrative set-up of the study area. Chapter three gives a thorough review of the existing literatures on the subject. Educational profile of the state and an account of the public expenditure on education are examined in the fourth chapter. Fifth chapter constitutes the core of the study, which devotes to the estimation and analysis of the per unit public and private cost of higher education. It discusses the related issues and components of recurring and non-recurring costs, subsidization of higher education, determination of optimum enrolment size in various institutions etc., at length. Chapter six enumerates the sources of fund for higher education and shows their relative importance. Finally, in the seventh chapter major findings are summarized which, if taken care of by the appropriate authority, will go a long way in solving the resource crisis of higher educational sector of the state.

I congratulate the author for his hard work. I hope the present work opens up new challenges and inspire further research while it answers old ones, enriching the available scanty literature on this emerging issue.

Aizawl
The 2nd June, 2012

Prof. Tlanglawma (Retd.)
Mizoram University, Aizawl

Preface

Education is an important factor in forming and sustaining human resources. This aspect of education has been given due importance since the second half of the last century. Like other factors, education is not costless. With the increase in population, mass consciousness, and all other kinds of advancement of society the demand for education has been ever increasing. This quantitative expansion of the education sector, along with the consideration of quality and equality, is bound to raise the demand for more funds and cause a greater entry of students at the tertiary level as higher education is viewed as the only means to augment the human resources.

With the increase in enrolment unless more resources are obtained, quality of education is sure to deteriorate. So, additional resource mobilization from public and private sources is inevitable. However, educational finance is of a distinct nature. Although public expenditure on education is seen to have been increasing, there are obvious restrictions on it. In this era of liberalization social sectors, including education, are being adversely affected. Moreover, emphasis is given more on the lower levels of education by the government and no exclusive mention is made of higher education as an independent sub-category. Further, under the new policy it is argued that higher education should be internalized and government should take care only of the elementary level, which in India is also a constitutional obligation. Thus, public expenditure on higher education is to be reduced. This indicates to the need of heavy reliance on private sources for higher educational finance, which is practically a difficult task in poor countries like India. As to the issue of equality it is questioned as to why higher education should be subsidized for all students across the board.

The situation in the small hilly State of Mizoram is more serious. Mizoram has very little resources of its own and a relatively large government sector. Education sector, especially higher education, faces an acute setback. In the literature of economics of education, cost and finance are often synonymously used. Since provision of more finance is difficult in the present case, cost reduction seems to be the viable way. Hence, in the present study a humble attempt has been made to analyze the public and private cost of higher education in Mizoram. It also examines the sources of fund for higher education in the state with their relative importance. The subject matter of the present book is of immense importance to the whole society comprising the students, teachers, researchers and policy makers of today with definite implications for the future generations too.

In spite of my best efforts, some errors and omissions may be noticed by the readers. I accept the responsibility of any such flaws and welcome constructive comments and suggestions for further improvement of the book.

Aizawl **Abdul Hannan Barbhuiya**
1st June, 2012

Acknowledgements

All praise to Almighty, the most merciful, the most beneficent who showered me the blessings of mental faculty and sound health to complete this work.

I, then, express my sincere thanks to Prof. Tlanglawma, who has written the foreword of the book. He has taken the pain in going through all the manuscripts and enriched the same with valuable suggestions.

The preparation of this book would not have been possible without the cooperation of the respondents who supplied the primary data for it. So, I am very much grateful to all of them. My thanks are due to the Principals/Heads, students and the staff of different higher educational institutions of the state, who generously supplied me the required information for this study. I also gratefully acknowledge the help received from the friends and colleagues in course of collecting data for the study.

I am also grateful to the officials of the State and the Central Governments who generously appreciated and provided me an easy access to their official records, books and other materials from which indispensable secondary information for the book was generated. I express my appreciation to the authorities of Directorate of Higher and Technical Education, Directorate of School Education, Directorate of Economics and Statistics, Directorate of Information and Public Relations, Directorate of Census Operations, Department of Finance, Planning and Programme Implementation Department, Mizoram Assembly Secretariat, Mizoram University, Aizawl, State

Library, Aizawl, Central Library, MZU, Maulana Azad Library, AMU, Chepauk Library, University of Madras and JNU Library, New Delhi.

My special thanks are due to Dr. James L.T. Thanga, Senior Statistical Assistant, Department of Economics, Mizoram University, for his crucial help with statistical analyses as and when asked for.

I am obliged to my Principal, Dr. B. Vanlalruala and other faculty members, especially the ones from the Department of Economics, Kamalanagar College for their cooperation and encouragement throughout my period of study.

The untiring efforts and sacrifice of my parents from the very day one of my life till date made me see this moment of achievement. Words may fail to appreciate their endeavour, so I thank them from the innermost corner of my heart. I am extremely grateful to my mother-in-law for her untainted inspiration and ceaseless prayers. So also, I appreciate the well wishes of my elder brother and brother-in-law.

Throughout the preparation of this book my wife Abida and my kids Alvi and Ismat had to bear a lot. I deeply express my heartfelt gratefulness to them, especially to my wife for her level best efforts to spare me for the study.

I received inexpressible assistance from the faculty members and staff of the Department of Economics, Mizoram University. Sincere thanks are due to them.

Finally, I convey my appreciation to the far and near authors, scholars and researchers whose works have been consulted and drawn upon during the course of this research work.

Aizawl
1st June, 2012

Abdul Hannan Barbhuiya

Contents

List of Tables

List of Figure

List of Maps

1

Introduction

Introduction

It is now generally believed that improvements in the quality of labour, acquired through education, training etc., can lead to higher rates of economic growth. In this sense, education happens to be the foremost factor of human capital formation and hence an important engine of economic growth. Along with its concept of human capital, economics of education has revolutionarised economic thinking and emerged as an independent discipline since the 1960s.

Economics of education has drawn for its own development heavily from Economics, and in turn influenced heavily the development of Economics and also the fast promising area of Development Studies (Tilak, 2008). Economics of education also broadened the scope of economic planning. The contributions in Economics of education during the last four and a half decades opened up new vistas in, and have influenced considerably and even expanded the boundaries of the theories of growth, labour market economics, public finance and development economics. Economics of education also entered the theories of social choice and even Welfare Economics. Further, it became an important area in public policy studies.

The subject matter of economics of education may broadly be categorized into: (i) education-development relationships, (ii) educational production function, and (iii) financing of education. In the present study, we concentrate on this third aspect, viz., the financing of education, which covers the principles of allocation of resources, mobilization of resources, public and private finance, household investment in education, cost of education etc.

The different aspects of education which require a detailed probe relate to how much a government needs to spend on education and how this expenditure is to be financed; is education mainly 'investment' or mainly 'consumption'; if investment, how much is the yield compared to other forms of investment; if consumption, what are the determinants of the demand for education. However, it is important to assess which form of education would serve the needs of the economy.

There has been found a positive correlation between education and level of development in different countries during different periods. These calculations confirmed, though in a general way, that education is a form of investment.

However, a good number of economists are not at comfort about the concept of human capital. Schultz feels that this is on account of "our values and beliefs which inhibit us from looking upon human beings as capital goods, except in slavery, and this we abhor" (Schultz, 1961). To consider man as wealth or as a marketable asset would reduce man to a mere material component, to something akin to property. For man to look upon himself as capital may seem to debase him. H.G. Shaffer (1961) criticizes the concept of human capital on the following grounds:

(a) Investment on man is essentially different from investment in non-human capital. A part of the expenditure for improvement of man is undertaken for reasons other than expectation of a monetary return, its effects on future output are uncertain and it satisfies wants directly. Further, it is inseparable from expenditure that may be termed as investment.
(b) It is virtually impossible to allocate specific return to a specific investment in man. Aggregate expenditure on improvements in man's skill and abilities, it is accepted does have a positive influence of "indeterminate magnitude" on man's efficiency and hence on output.
(c) Even if it were possible to separate consumption expenditure

> from investment expenditure in man, and income from such investment could be computed, as a basis for public policy it would be of questionable value.

In the area of financing of education, the trends in India correspond with the global trends – high rates of growth in public expenditure on education in the 1960s, negative rates of growth in the 1970s, steady but slow positive growth in the 1980s, and declining growth in the 1990s that accompanied the 'Structural Adjustment Policies' (SAPs). A look into the impact of structural adjustment on educational financing would reveal that adjustment is associated with a decline in: (i) public financing of education, (ii) gross primary enrolment rates, (iii) teacher-student ratio, and (iv) the growth of teachers. Our concern, however, in this study is in the constraints to financing.

In the case of Mizoram, the state government adopted a policy of subsidizing higher education and provided liberal grants-in-aid, since statehood. However, around 1990, the system of state financing of higher education came under severe constraints and now education is being considered as a 'merit good' and privatization of higher education is being advocated. It has added yet another dimension to the problem under consideration.

The present study concentrates on the various aspects of cost and financing of higher education in Mizoram encompassing general, professional and technical education. The cases of primary and secondary education were taken up as and when necessary, which, however, are outside the purview of this study.

Education and Economic Development

The interrelationship between education and economic development can be traced back to the pen of Plato, much earlier than the formal birth of Economics as an independent branch of knowledge. Then, starting from Adam Smith, the father of Economics, a long tradition of classical and neo-classical economists emphasized the role of education in economic development. However, due attention was given to the area only since the second half of the twentieth century. The year 1960 marks the beginning of a new era when, in fact, a formal area of study, viz., Economics of Education was born with the Presidential Address by Theodore W. Schultz to the American Economic Association in December 1960 on "Investment in Human Capital".

Role of Education in Economic Development

From theoretical viewpoint, there are at least three mechanisms through which education may affect economic growth. First, education increases the human capital inherent in the labour force, which increases labour productivity and thus transitional growth towards a higher equilibrium level of output. Second, education may increase the innovative capacity of the economy, and the new knowledge on technologies, products and processes, which promotes growth. Third, education may facilitate the diffusion and transmission of knowledge needed to understand and process new information and to successfully implement new technologies devised by others, which again promotes economic growth.

For a positive change in the society and sustained economic growth education plays a pivotal role. Primary education helps in removing stranglehold of traditions which characterize the society in under developed countries that are inimical to growth and development. Secondary education provides the base for higher and technical education. Higher education prepares the manpower for higher cadre posts both in the public and in the private sector. Thus, education breaks the vicious circle of ignorance, dogmatism and stagnation, and brings in productivity by way of enhancing scientific temper in students and inculcating in them the urge to innovate, to develop, to progress, all of which ensure a better standard of living.

Benefits of education may be direct and indirect, social or private, tangible or intangible. Generally speaking, direct benefits are private, i.e. they are enjoyed by the individuals in the form of higher earnings, occupational flexibility, better status, cultural refinement etc. Indirect benefits are enjoyed both by the individuals as well as by the society. An enlightened population willing to accept new ideas, new challenges, greater tolerance which goes to ease communal tensions, improvement in social and cultural levels, promotion of democratic values, positive thinking and behaviour of people, productive use and enjoyment of leisure are some of the spill-over benefits to society which are at the samc time enjoyed by the individuals as well. These intangible benefits, though not amenable to measurement, have a powerful effect on society and on the economy. It creates the right type of environment, which promotes development in the economy. In fact, it is these changes which bring out the difference between economic growth and economic development, since 'development' encompasses both 'growth' and 'change'.

Contribution of Education to Economic Development

There has been a revival of interest in the concept of investment in human capital which developed in the United States and the United Kingdom in the late 1950s and early 1960s that resulted into tremendous growth of research and publication concerning the question of the relationship between education and the economy.

An American economist, Edward F. Denison (1962) conducted a study in this regard and concluded his analysis that, increases in the level of education of the labour force accounted for as much as 23 per cent of the annual rate of growth of GNP in the United States between 1930 and 1960. Russian economist Strumillin (1925) estimated that, education at primary and elementary level resulted in as much as 79 per cent increase in the output and wage of a labourer in the erstwhile Soviet Union. Schultz (1961) analyzed the contribution of education to growth in national income in the United States from 1900 to 1956 and came to the conclusion that, investment in education contributed 3.5 times more to the increase in gross national income than investment in physical capital. A World Bank Study of 192 countries concluded that, "only 16 per cent of the growth is explained by physical capital (machinery, buildings and physical infrastructure), while 20 per cent comes from natural capital. But not less than 64 per cent can be attributed to human and social capital (HDR, 1966).

Thus, Mark Blaug (1972) rightly observed that, "The universality of this positive association between education and earnings is one of the most striking findings of modern social science. It is indeed one of the few safe generalizations that one can make about labour markets in all countries whether capitalist or communist."

Approaches to Education and Economic Development

Different attempts by different economists were made to estimate the contribution of education to economic development, which may broadly be classified into the following approaches:

Simple Correlation Approach

In this approach an attempt is made to correlate some index of educational activity with some index of the level of economic activity. The levels of literacy and per capita incomes of different countries may be compared with each other to find out that level of literacy which will help in achieving a high rate of growth. Similarly, any other index like percentage of GNP spent on education may be correlated to per capita GNP or level of education to per capita income. Names attached to this approach are: of Anderson and Bowman (1963), Harbison and Myers (1964), McClelland (1966), Lockheed (1987), Hicks (1987), Mukherjee and Rao (1967), Chaudhuri (1969) and Ansari (1987,1993).

Residual Approach

Increase in total national income of an economy over a given period of time is examined under this approach allowing for the contribution of measurable inputs, such as capital and labour, and concludes that the residual is attributable to the unspecified inputs. Among the unspecified inputs, education and advances in knowledge are the most important. E.F. Denison (1962), the chief exponent of this approach, used the Cobb-Douglas production function in calculating the value of the residual factor for U.S.A. for the period 1927 to 1957. The average growth rate during the period could not be accounted for by the contribution of the factors of production, namely land, labour and capital. The average growth rate worked out to be 2.9 per cent and the value of the residue was little more than 2 per cent, which according to him was on account of advancement of knowledge. This formed the basis of the 'residual approach' and along these lines other important contributors are Abromovitz (1957), Solow (1957), Kendrick (1961), and Schultz (1961).

Returns to Education Approach

Returns to education may be direct and indirect, the former being quantifiable and the latter are not amenable to measurement. Generally, direct monetary returns are taken into account in the calculation of rates of returns to education. Indirect returns may be in the form of an enlightened electorate, greater tolerance among people, hence fewer frictions, and therefore, an amicable and conducive environment in which development can take place. It has been found that education yields a high rate of return on investment. The monetary returns in the form of lifetime earnings to the individual far exceed the cost of education. The rate of return approach is of use in assessing the contribution of education to economic growth. It is equally useful in determining how much is to be invested in education *vis-à-vis* other sectors of the economy. This approach though theoretically sound has been criticized on the grounds of considering non-economic intangible benefits of education and the difficulty in obtaining accurate data to calculate the returns attributable to education. Economists using this approach are Becker (1975), Hauthakker (1959), Psacharopolos (1981), Hussain (1967), Panchemukhi (1969) and Tilak (1987).

Manpower Planning Approach

For economic development modern economies require a wide range of human skills and knowledge acquired by manpower. In fact, it is impossible to utilize efficiently many of the complex forms of physical capital in the absence of a relatively high level of human skills. Manpower Planning Approach tries to give a rough estimate of the future requirements of educated and skilled manpower of an economy for different productive sectors. Some of the techniques and methods adopted for projecting manpower requirements include. (a) estimation on the basis of the employers' opinion about their future manpower requirements; (b) extrapolation of the past employment trends into the future (Harbison and Myers, 1974); (c) inter-country comparisons (OECD, 1962); (d) on the basis of Development Plans and Projects, and (e) on the basis of productivity of labour and future output (Parnes,

1964). Some important contributors to this approach are Correa-Tinbergen-Bos (1964), Leyard and Saigal (1966), Stone (1966), Ramanujan (1969), Shri Prakash (1971, 1977), Prakash and Radhakrishnan (1973) and Lawma (1990).

Linkage Between Education and Economic Development

That Education and Economic Development are positively related is a known fact. The association between the two can be seen under the following linkages:

Quantitative Linkage

Adult literacy rates or school enrolment ratios were taken as proxies for the human capital of an economy in the early days. Then the shift was on average years of schooling. Finally, Barro and Lee (1993) provided for internationally comparable data on average years of schooling. In essence, more schooling is associated with higher individual earnings. However, social returns could be either above or below the private returns. The most common argument is that, the social returns will exceed the private returns because of the positive effects of education on crime, health, fertility and on growth and productivity of the economy as a whole.

Qualitative Linkage

Ignoring quality differences significantly distorts the picture about the relationship between education and economic outcomes. Much of the discussion of quality has identified cognitive skills, such as mathematics and science, as the important dimension. Hanushek and Kim find a statistically and economically significant positive effect of the quality of education on economic growth. They, in a study observe that, immigrants who were schooled in countries that have higher scores in the international mathematics and science examinations earn more in the United States. Thus, it is not simply the quality of education, rather quality education which contributes more to economic growth and development.

Institutional Linkage

The effect of educational quality on economic growth may differ depending on the economic institution of a country. The pace of economic growth depends to a great extent upon the availability and quality of economic institutions. It is hard to have a strongly growing economy without complementary institutions in the labour and product markets, without openness to trade and investment and without effective systems of laws and property rights. Deficiencies in the institutional environment result into misuse of cognitive skills rendering the average effect of education on growth negligible.

Financial Linkage

Since cost of education is considered to be investment expenditure rather than consumption expenditure, adequate financing of this strategically important sector can only lead to a faster growth and lasting development of an economy. In the area of financing of education, the trends in India correspond with the global trends – high rates of growth in public expenditure on education in the 1960s, negative rates of growth in the 1970s, steady but slow positive growth in the 1980s and declining growth in the 1990s that accompanied the adjustment policies.

To sum up, the mutually reinforcing relationship between education and economic development can be witnessed both at macro and micro levels. At macro level, nations with illiterate and less educated masses cannot progress or increase their output substantially and as a result remain at low standards of living. At the micro level, illiterate and less educated individuals or households are less productive, join less paying occupations, thus earn less and remain at very low levels of living, mostly below poverty line. As to the efficacy of education, APJ Abdul Kalam rightly states that, "Education is the engine of economic growth and social change. It creates motivation for progress and brings revolution in the ideas necessary for the progress of the country. It teaches honesty, inspires patriotism, enhances social prestige and promotes economic development. When people are educated, we not only get teachers, professionals and executives but more importantly citizens who are aware, sensitive and responsible. It makes people place social good above personal gains. Not only this, it transforms a human being into a whole sole whole, a noble soul and an asset to the universe."

Importance of the Study

During the last five decades or so the priority which was earlier given to investment in physical capital for effecting economic growth has changed and emphasis is now on human capital, which constitutes human resources capable of yielding economic returns over their life span. Investment in human capital may take several forms, the most important being investment in education.

Like other producing units, educational institutions transform inputs into outputs, incurring costs in the process. The inputs of educational plants consist of both the human and physical resources. These factor inputs comprise the services of teachers and other non-teaching staff as human inputs, inputs of students' time and services as raw-materials, services of the means of transportation and communications and services of such material goods as books, stationery and uniforms, buildings, laboratory and other equipments as physical inputs of the educational production. The identification of the unit of output in education is a typical problem. Enrolments are generally taken as the output of education in order to estimate unit cost of education. The output of education may be said to be the "knowledge added" or "educational value added" which consist of the knowledge acquired and capabilities developed by the students at each stage of their education. Total enrolment is taken as gross output and the number of passed-out or graduates may be regarded as net output (Prakash, 1996).

The services of the factor inputs of education are purchased from different markets. The size of the markets of individual input may be spread from purely local to international and their structures may be approximated from pure competition to near perfect monopoly. However, most of the markets are highly specialized oligopolistic markets with widely differentiated products. The educational institutions which buy the factor services has to pay fixed prices set by the public authority in case of academic and non-academic staff while the services of other physical inputs at the prevailing market prices. In centrally planned economies, prices are fixed by government while prices are the result of the interplay of the forces of demand and supply in market economies (Prakash, 1996). Estimation and analysis of factor cost of education is done by classifying these factor inputs into different components, which enables the assessment of their level of utilization.

The economic significance of education has led to the allocation of a large proportion of public fund to the development of education, especially in developing countries. In India, like many other developing countries, national commitment was made in the field of education after Independence. Tremendous growth of education sector is seen in India because of consistent effort made under Five Year Plans. In the sphere of higher education, there were 25 university level institutions, 700 colleges, 15,000 teachers and 1,00,000 students in 1950, which has increased to 431 university level institutions, 20,677 colleges, 5,05,000 teachers, and 1,16,12,000 students by the year 2008 (Reddy, 2009). Thus, there is an ever expanding demand for education. India has the third largest higher education system in the world after China and the United States.

The magnificent growth of educational sector in the country absorbs a considerable amount of the national investible resources resulting in a serious resource crunch due to its limited share in public budget and a competition for resources with other sectors of the economy. Higher education in the pre-Independence days was largely supported by private charity. However, the role of government gradually increased in its financing after Independence, and public expenditure on education is seen to increase rapidly and steadily over the period. It increased from ₹ 114 crores in 1950-51 to ₹ 41978.21 crores in 2008-09, measured in current prices (Shaikh, 2009). This shows that expenditure incurred by public authorities has risen by nearly 368 times during the said period. In case of Mizoram, the budget expenditure on higher education has increased by 3.6 times, i.e. from ₹ 1161.88 lakhs in 1999-2000 to ₹ 4122.05 lakhs in 2008-09 (Table 4.9). However, the ratio of higher educational expenditure to the state budget and the Net State Domestic Product (NSDP) remained at 1.5 – 2.60 per cent and 0.82 – 2.03 per cent, respectively during the same period (Table 4.10). As to the sources of finance, the contribution of public sources increased from 87.3 per cent to 91.6 per cent during the period 1976-77 to 2007-08, while the share of private sources came down from 12.7 per cent to 8.4 per cent during the same period (Table 6.7). This implies a heavier burden on the shoulder of the government.

In fact, the public authority will find it difficult to earmark more of its revenue resources for the development of education, particularly higher education as the factors like increase in population, urbanization, improvement in economic standard, social and cultural consciousness etc., are pushing up the demand for education. In order to meet this increasing demand for education with the available limited resources, planners and policy makers will have to evolve methods for lowering the costs of education for a given level of output or increase the productivity of given inputs.

To devise effective strategies for achieving higher educational goals with limited resources it is necessary to have thorough studies on the various aspects of educational finance. Often in the study of financing of education 'cost' is taken synonymous to 'financing' on the assumption that financing is attempted to defray the costs. Analysis of costs is an integral part of educational management. Not only does it give us an idea of the total requirement of funds in the educational sector, it also gives us the extent of burden of educational expenditure on the government, how we can justify this expenditure in a poor country like India where many areas are in want of government's attention. Is it possible or desirable to shift a part of the burden to individuals? If so, how much of the burden can be shifted? These are relevant aspects which need to be examined. Besides this, unit cost can also be calculated. Educational costs per student or per course or per institution is required to work out financial allocations and costing of educational schemes to study the efficiency level of an institution, to improve the optimum utilization of resources and to evaluate the input-output design (Natarajan, 1990). Unit cost estimation has much practical significance in the field of educational planning. It serves as an important technique of evaluating the internal and external efficiency of resources invested in education.

The financing of education has been an area of attraction to the researchers and policy makers all over the world. Quite a few studies on financing of higher education at the national, state and micro level have been done in India by individual researchers, commissions and committees. To the best of our knowledge, except the one, "Higher Education in North-East India" by Vanlalchhawna in 2006, no other systematic study has been conducted in this field. The present study is an earnest attempt to analyze and examine the important aspects of financing higher education in Mizoram.

Objectives of the Study

Being the apex of entire educational structure, higher education plays an important part in the educational system of a country or a region. At the same time, it produces efficient manpower and promotes economic development. Higher educational history of Mizoram begins with the year 1958 when the first college was established in the state, with a substantial financial donation from the then philanthropist, Pu Pachhunga. During the decades of 1970s and 1990s there has been a rapid growth of higher educational institutions in the state. Initially, colleges were established basing on needs, but later on political considerations resulted into mushroom growth of colleges. This not only deteriorates the quality of higher education (as these institutions lack adequate infrastructural facilities) but also implies a greater financial burden on the state government. Therefore, the following objectives were set in the present study to make it not only of academic interest but also of practical utility:

1. To examine the growth of higher education in Mizoram with inter-district analysis.
2. To study the trend and pattern of public expenditure on education in the state.
3. To estimate per unit public and private cost of higher education in the study area.
4. To determine the optimum enrolment size in the higher educational institutions of Mizoram.
5. To analyze the sources of finance for higher education with their relative importance.

Hypotheses

The following hypotheses were postulated for empirical verification in the study:

1. There is an inverse relationship between unit cost and enrolment size.
2. Public cost per unit is higher than per unit private cost of higher education.
3. Higher education is highly subsidized in Mizoram.

Methodology and Database

In the present study, financing of higher education is analyzed by categorizing the higher educational institutions of Mizoram into three groups, viz. (1) general degree colleges, (2) professional colleges, and (3) technical institutions. In the absence of any technical institution offering degree courses and due to the joint management of higher and technical education by the same department of the state government, the two Polytechnics were included in the third group as 'technical institutions'. Data were also collected from Mizoram University and ICFAI University, Mizoram for post-graduate level of study. Apart from these, data were collected from several published as well as unpublished records of the government departments and other relevant secondary sources.

The unit cost of higher education in Mizoram is analyzed under two heads: (a) public cost, and (b) private cost. In the general discussion on public cost Mizoram University, and ICFAI University were not included since these two universities are still at their formative stage. Due to heavy capital expenditure and small student population, unit costs per student, in these universities worked out to be very high and hence are treated as statistical out layers. However, in the calculation of private cost of education the two universities were not excluded since only the expenditures directly borne by the students and their parents were taken into account in this case.

Composition and trend of unit cost of higher education were analyzed for the period 1997-98 to 2007-08. Analysis of the pattern and structure of per unit public cost of higher education for Mizoram followed by the pattern and structure of the same for the three types of higher educational intitutions separately were provided in the study. As for the private cost of higher education, it was analyzed for the academic year 2007-08.

In the analysis of data, simple statistics like percentage, means, standard deviation (SD), coefficient of variation (CV) and regression analysis were used. Proportionate or percentage shares of expenditure on individual items in the total cost were used in the analysis of public cost of higher education. Mean, standard deviation, maxima and minima were employed in analyzing the components of private cost. Coefficient of variation has been applied for showing the variation and variability of private cost of education.

For studying the relationship between unit cost and enrolment the former has been regressed on the latter using the Ordinary Least Square (OLS) method. The linear equation used is:

$$Y = b_0 + b_1 X \tag{1.1}$$

where Y = Unit Cost of Higher Education; and X = Enrolment. In the regression equation 'b_0' is Y intercept and 'b_1' is the regression coefficient which shows the rate of change in the cost per student for a unit change in enrolment. The strength of the relationship between the dependent variable Y and the independent variable X has been measured by the coefficient of determination (R^2).

Quadratic function had been fitted to the cost-enrolment data in order to determine the optimum enrolment size and the minimum cost corresponding to it. The second degree polynomial function used is:

$$Y = b_0 + b_1 X + b_2 X^2 \tag{1.2}$$

where Y = Unit Cost of Higher Education; X = Enrolment; and b_0, b_1 and b_2 are the constants of the function. The optimum enrolment or the minimum unit cost was determined by following the simple optimization techniques of calculus as follows:

First Order Condition: $dy/dx = 0$ (1.3)

Second Order Condition: $d^2y/dx^2 > 0$; Minimum (1.4)

< 0; Maximum

Calculation of Public Cost

Public cost of higher education (PBC) is the sum total of the expenditure on recurring (RC) and non-recurring (NRC) heads incurred by the public authority.

$$PBC = RC + NRC \quad (1.5)$$

Per unit public cost (PBUC) is obtained by dividing the public cost (PBC) by the number of students enrolled (N).

$$PBUC = PBC/N \quad (1.6)$$

Recurring cost (RC) has again been classified into the expenditure on salary, DA, etc., (SD), building (repairs etc.) (BD), maintenance of furniture (FR), library maintenance (LB), scholarship (SC), laboratory (LT), student activities (SA), telephone/internet (TI), travelling allowances (TA), and other stuff (OS).

$$RC = SD + BD + FR + LB + SC + LT + SA + TI + TA + OS \quad (1.7)$$

Likewise, non-recurring cost (NRC) consists of expenditure on library (new addition to or asset creation in) (LB), construction (CN), equipment (EQ), furniture (new addition) (FR), and other items (OI).

$$NRC = LB + CN + EQ + FR + OI \quad (1.8)$$

Net public cost per unit (NPBUC) is calculated by deducting the admission fee, tuition fee and other non-refundable fees (FE) from the total public cost (PBC) divided by the number of students enrolled (N).

$$NPBUC = (PBC–FE)/N \quad (1.9)$$

Calculation of Private Cost

Private cost of higher education (PVC) is calculated by adding up the expenditures borne directly by the students and their parents on admission, tuition and other non-refundable fees (FE), books, stationery, internet etc. (BS), accommodation (AM), food including tiffin (FD), conveyance (CY), and personal maintenance such as healthcare sports etc. (PM).

$$PVC = FE + BS + AM + FD + CY + PM \qquad (1.10)$$

Per unit private cost (PVUC) is calculated by dividing the private cost (PVC) by the number of students enrolled (N).

$$PVUC = PVC/N \qquad (1.11)$$

Net private cost per unit (NPVUC) was found out by subtracting the amount of scholarship received by each student (SC/N) from the per unit private cost (PVUC).

$$NPVUC = PVUC-SC/N \qquad (1.12)$$

Sample Size and Selection of Sample Units

In the process of generating empirical data for this study multi-stage (two-stage) sampling was adopted. In the first stage, 15 out of 22 general degree colleges were selected. Colleges were selected in such a way that– (i) both rural and urban areas are represented, (ii) colleges with high, low and medium size of enrolment are included, and (iii) at least one college from each district is covered. As for the professional colleges, 1 out of 3, located in Aizawl city, was taken as the sample. As the other two colleges impart training mostly to the employees, Mizoram Law College was selected as the sample. Regarding technical institutions, both the Polytechnics of the state were selected, one each from Aizawl and Lunglei district. For the cost of post-graduate level of education, the sole central university, i.e. Mizoram University and the sole private university, i.e. ICFAI University, Mizoram were taken as the sample.

In the second stage, students were stratified course-wise from the sample institutions and then selected, at random, from each stratum. Number of students selected randomly from each course was as follows: 84 from BA, 36 from B.Sc., 18 from B.Com., 10 from LLB, 24 from technical courses, 12 from MA, 14 from M.Sc., 6 from M.Com., 4 from BE, 3 from MBA, 3 from BBA, 3 from BCA, and 3 from BHTM. In all, 220 students out of the total enrolment of 7254, representing 3.03 per cent, were selected to constitute the sample.

Procedure of Data Collection

Data for the present study were collected both from the primary and the secondary sources. However, for cost analysis, the required data were mainly collected from primary sources. For this purpose three sets of questionnaires were prepared and administered.

The first set consists of the Questionnaire to the Directorate of Higher and Technical Education. General information on colleges and technical institutions with enrolment and financial aspects at the state level was collected through this questionnaire.

Questionnaires to the Higher Educational/Technical Institutions were the second set, through which data were collected on institutional details like personnel strength, student strength, examination performance, and more emphatically on costs – recurring and non-recurring, and the various sources of finance.

The third set of questionnaires was the once designed to obtain information from the students. For private cost of education this was the only means, which collected the students' personal, socio-economic, expenditure related, income related and borrowing related data.

Secondary data were also collected from published and unpublished sources of government departments like Directorate of Census Operations, Directorate of Economics and Statistics, Planning and Programme Implementation Department, Finance Department of Mizoram and various websites of the state government, central government and international organizations.

Cost of Higher Education at Current and Constant Prices

Finally, the time series data on cost of higher education at (market) current prices of our present study were converted into constant prices using the Wholesale Price Index (WPI) with the base year 1993-94 (=100). In doing so, the WPI figure for 'All Commodities' were taken into consideration.

Limitations of the Study

Against lofty blue-prints researchers usually come across several constraints and barriers. The present work is also not an exception. The main limitations of the study are:

(i) The opportunity cost of education could not be estimated. In the absence of opportunity cost or income foregone by the students, total cost of education consists of public cost and direct private cost.

(ii) Expenditure on direction and administration at the Directorate and Secretariat level were not included in the estimation of cost of education at the undergraduate level. However, the administrative costs were included in the case of post graduate level of study.

(iii) Data on public cost could practically be collected for only ten years in spite of the fact that questionnaires for this purpose were designed for twenty years. Similarly, in the process of collecting data on private cost from the students a good number of questionnaires had to be rejected on the ground of incomplete and dubious response.

(iv) All aspects relating to the financing of higher education in the state could not be covered in the present study leaving scope for further research in the field.

Scheme of Chapters

The present study is divided into the following seven chapters:

- Chapter 1 deals with a brief introduction of the topics, interrelationship between education and economic development, scope and objectives, importance of the study, limitations, hypotheses, methodology and scheme of chapters.
- Chapter 2 provides a brief profile of the State including its location and area, topography and climate, resource base, flora and fauna, socio-cultural background, administrative set-up, population profile, political history and economic scene.
- Chapter 3 presents a brief review of literatures on the subject at local, regional, national and international levels.

- Chapter 4 examines the profile of educational development in Mizoram with inter-district comparisons and growth trend of public expenditure on education, in general and higher education, in particular.
- Chapter 5 analyses the estimates of per unit public and private costs with their components, and the estimates of net and total cost of higher education in Mizoram. It also shows the relationship between unit cost and enrolment, and attempts to determine the optimum enrolment size for different types of institutions.
- Chapter 6 discusses the different sources of finance for higher education in the State with their relative significance.
- Chapter 7 finally presents the summary of major findings and conclusion.

REFERENCES

Annual Plans, (1997-98 to 2007-08), *Planning and Programme Implementation Department*, Government of Mizoram, Aizawl.

Annual Report (2007-08), Mizoram University, Aizawl.

Barro, R.J. and Lee, J.W (1993) International Comparisons of Educational Attainment, *Journal of Monetary Economics*, 32, 3.

Blaug, Mark (1970), "*An Introduction to Economics of Education*", London: Allen Lane the Penguin.

Denison, E.F., (1962), "The Sources of Economic Growth in the United States and the Alternatives Before Us"; *Committee for Economic Development*, New York.

Economic Survey, Mizoram, (2008-09), Planning & Programme Implementation Department, Government of Mizoram, Aizawl.

Government of India: Office of the Economic Adviser, Ministry of Commerce and Industry, New Delhi.

Kalam, A.P.J. (2005), President's Address to the Nation on the Eve of Independence Day, 2004, published in *Yojana*, September.

Nagarjuna, B. and Narayana, D.L. (2005), *Economics of Human Resource Development: A Perspective Analysis*, Serials Publication, New Delhi.

Natarajan, S. (1990), *Introduction to Economics of Education*, Sterling Publications, New Delhi.

Prakash, S. (1996), 'Optimisation in Resource Use in Elementary Education in India' in Koti, K.R. *et al.,* (ed.) *Studies in Indian Economy* (Prof. P.R. Mathur Memorial volume), Himalaya Publishing House, Bombay.

Rao, V.K.R.V. (1966), *Socio-economic Survey of Greater Delhi City*, Asia Publishing House.

Reddy, D.N. and Kishore, K.L. (2009): 'Revamping Higher Education: Need of the Hour', *University News*, 47 (45), November 9-15.

Schultz, T.W. (1961) "Investment in Human Capital", *American Economic Review*, 51(1) March.

Shaffer, H.G. (1961), "Investment in Human Capital: Comment", *American Economic Review*, Vol. 52, No. 4

Shaikh, S. and Gawali, V. (2009): 'Does India Need Foreign Universities?' *University News*, 47 (39), September 28-October 4.

Statistical Abstract of Mizoram (2007), Directorate of Economics and Statistics, Government of Mizoram, Aizawl.

Statistical Handbook of Mizoram (2008), Directorate of Economics and Statistics, Government of Mizoram, Aizawl.

Strumillin, S.G. (1925), Economic Significance of National Education, Reprinted in "*The Economics of Education*" (eds. Robinson, E.A.G., Vaizey, J.), London, Macmillan, 1966.

Tilak, J.B.G. (2008), 'Economics of Human Capital in India' in *Economics of Education and Health in India* (ed.) A.K. Thakur and Md. A. Salam, Deep and Deep Publications Pvt. Ltd., New Delhi.

Vanlalchhawna (2006), *Higher Education in North East India*, Mittal Publications, New Delhi.

2

Mizoram – A Brief Profile

Introduction

The growth of any economy, through its various stages of development, influences education which, in turn, influences the development process. All aspects of the society have an impact on the system of education. The values, it stands for and the pangs undergone in socio-cultural economic and political development, all have a bearing on education in general and higher education, in particular. The present chapter gives an overview of Mizoram from its geographical, topographical, geological, socio-cultural, administrative, demographic, political and economic perspective.

Location and Area

Mizoram became the 23rd State of the Indian Union on 20th February, 1987. It was one of the districts (Lushai Hills district) of Assam till 21st January, 1972 when it became Union Territory. Sandwiched between Myanmar in the east and south and Bangladesh in the west, Mizoram occupies an area of great strategic importance in the southernmost corner of North-East India.

The State covers a total area of 21,081 sq. kms. The length of the state from north to south is about 277 kms and the width from east to west is about 121 kms. Mizoram is bounded on the north by Cachar district of Assam and the state of Manipur, on the east and south by

Myanmar (Burma), and on the west by Bangladesh and the state of Tripura. Mizoram shares an international boundary of 722 kms, i.e. 404 kms with Myanmar and 318 kms with Bangladesh, while it has an inter-state border of 495 kms comprising 123 kms with Assam, 277 kms with Tripura and 95 kms with Manipur. The state is geographically located between 21.58° to 24.35° N latitude and 92.15° to 93.29° E longitude. The tropic of cancer runs through the territory.

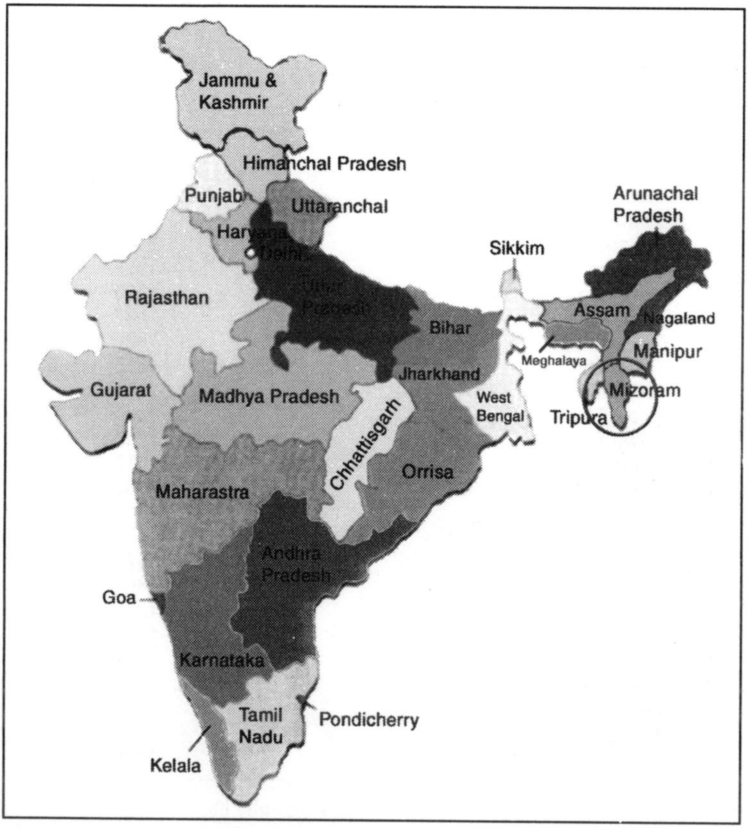

Map 2.1: Location of Mizoram in India

Topography

Mizoram has the most dappled topography among all hilly areas in this part of the country. It is a land of rolling hills, rivers and lakes.

The hill ranges of Mizoram are in sharp contrast with the major mountain ranges of the country. They run north to south and tend to grow higher in the eastern side and taper off to the north and south. The hills are extremely rocky and steep and the ranges leave some plains scattered occasionally here and there. The average height of the hills is about 900 metres.

As many as 23 major hills ranges or peaks of different heights run through the length and breadth of the state. Table 2.1 shows the various mountains of Mizoram with their heights above the sea level.

Table 2.1: Mountains of Mizoram

Sl. No.	*Name of mountain*	*Height (in metres)*
1.	Phawngpui (Blue Mountain)	2157
2.	Lengteng	2141
3.	Surtlang	1967
4.	Lurhtlang	1935
5.	Tan Tlang	1837
6.	V. Partlang	1929
7.	Chalhfilh Tlang	1865
8.	Hrangturzotlang	1854
9.	Zopui Tlang	1850
10.	Tawizo	1837
11.	Mawmrang	1812
12.	Purun Tlang	1756
13.	Hmuifangtlang	1619
14.	Saireptlang	1555
15.	Sakawrhmutuaitlang	1535
16.	Reiek Tlang	1465
17.	Thorang Tlang	1387.2
18.	Buia Hmun Tlang	1383
19.	Laipui Tlang	1188
20.	South Hlimen Tlang	1179
21.	Head Post Office	1067.7
22.	Serkawn	1222
23.	Circuit House (Lunglei)	1105.3

Source: http://www.mizoram.nic/about/physiography.htm

Although many rivers and streamlets drain the hill ranges, the most important and useful rivers are the Tlawng (also known as Dhaleswari or Katakhal), Tut (Gutur), Tuirial (Sonai), Serlui (Rukni) and Tuivawl which flow through the northern territory and eventually join river Barak in Cachar district of Assam.

The Koldoyne (Chhimtuipui) which originates in Myanmar, is an important river in the south Mizoram. It has four tributaries and the river is in patches. The western part is drained by Karnaphuli (Khawthlang tuipui) and its tributaries. A number of important towns including Chittagong in Bangladesh is situated at the mouth of the river. Before Independence, access to other parts of the country was possible only through the river routes *via* Cachar in the north, and *via* Chittagong in the south. Entry through the later was sealed when the Subcontinent was partitioned and ceded to East Pakistan (now Bangladesh) in 1947.

Table 2.2 lists out the important rivers of Mizoram with their length in kilometres.

Table 2.2: Main Rivers of Mizoram

Sl. No.	*Name of River*	*Length in Kms*
1.	Tlawng	185.15
2.	Tlau	159.39
3.	Chhimtuipui (Koladyne)	138.46
4.	Khawthlangtuipui (R.Karnaphuli)	128.08
5.	Tuichang	120.75
6.	Tuirial	117.53
7.	Tuichawng	107.87
8.	Mat	90.16
9.	Tuipui	86.94
10.	Tuivawl	72.45
11.	Teirei	70.84
12.	Tuirini	59.57
13.	Serlui	56.33

Source: http://www.mizoram.nic/about/physiography.htm

Lakes are scattered all over the state. But the most important of them are Palak, Tamdil, Rungdil and Rengdil. The Palak lake is situated in Chhimtuipui District in southern Mizoram and covers an area of 30 Ha. It is believed that the lake was created as a result of an earthquake or a flood. The Tamdil lake is a natural lake situated 110 kms from Aizawl. The common man belief is that there was once a huge mustard plant in this place. When the plant was cut off, jets of water sprayed from the plant created a pool of water, and thus the name Tamdil which means 'Lake of Mustard Plant' was born. Today the lake is an important tourist attraction and a holiday resort. The Rungdil lake occupies an area of 2.5 hectares is a combination of two lakes lying side by side separated by a narrow strip of land.

Climate

The climate of Mizoram is moderate, cool and pleasant throughout the year. It is generally cool in summer and not very cold in winter. The temperature varies from 20°-30°C during summer, 11°-21°C during winter and the relative humidity varies from 70-80%.

The upper parts of the hills are, predictably cold, cool during the summer, while the lower reaches are relatively warm and humid. Storms break out during March-April, just before or around the summer. The maximum average temperature in the summer is 30°C while in the winter the minimum average temperature is around 11°C. Winter in Mizoram is wonderfully blue, and in the enchanting view of wide stretches of a vast lake of cloud. The four months between November and February are winter in Mizoram which is followed by the spring. The storms come in the middle of April to herald the beginning of the summer. The mercury starts rising and the hills come under the cover of a haze. The three months from June to August are known as the rainy season. With a temperature ranging between 19°C and 24°C, the climate is at its moderate best in the two autumnal months of September and October.

The entire area of the State is under the direct influence of the monsoon. Mizoram receives south-west and north-east monsoon. Generally, it rains during May to September. However, July and August are the two months during which Mizoram receives the heaviest rainfall.

The average rainfall in the state was about 2514.80 mm per annum during the period 2001 to 2005. Table 2.3 presents the average annual rainfall in Mizoram for the period 2001-2005.

Rainfall is seen not to vary much across different parts of the state. The average rainfall in the district headquarters of Mizoram for the period 2001 to 2005 is given in Table 2.4. The table shows that, except Champhai, rainfall is almost evenly distributed among all the districts of Mizoram.

Table 2.3: Average Annual Rainfall in Mizoram (2002-2005)

Sl. No.	*Year*	*Rainfall (in mm)*
1.	2001	2535
2.	2002	2648
3.	2003	2546
4.	2004	2751
5.	2005	2094

Source: *Statistical Handbook of Mizoram*, 2006.

Table 2.4: Average Rainfall in District Headquarters of Mizoram (2001-2005)

(In mm)

Sl. No.	*Name of Station*	*Year*				
		2001	2002	2003	2004	2005
1.	Aizawl	2401	2568	2815	2581	2113
2.	Kolasib	4204	3117	2866	2830	2537
3.	Mamit	2317	2703	2513	2828	2056
4.	Lunglei	3641	3505	3382	4076	2773
5.	Champhai	1632	1842	1792	2032	1650
6.	Serchhip	2253	2506	2746	2588	1424
7.	Lawngtlai	2144	3203	2771	2440	2461
8.	Saiha	2132	2762	2501	2570	2437

Source: Same as Table 2.3.

Resource Base

Resource base of Mizoram has been divided into three 'resource association regions' taking into account all the tangible parameters which together form the resource, and which also reflect the intangible aspects of the resource in its totality (Kumar, 2003).

As per the above categorization of parameters, the Blockwise resource associations of Mizoram have been shown in Table 2.5.

Out of the total resources, the percentage contribution by natural resources, human resources and cultural resources is presented in Table 2.6.

Flora and Fauna

The hilly state of Mizoram is very rich in terms of flora and fauna.

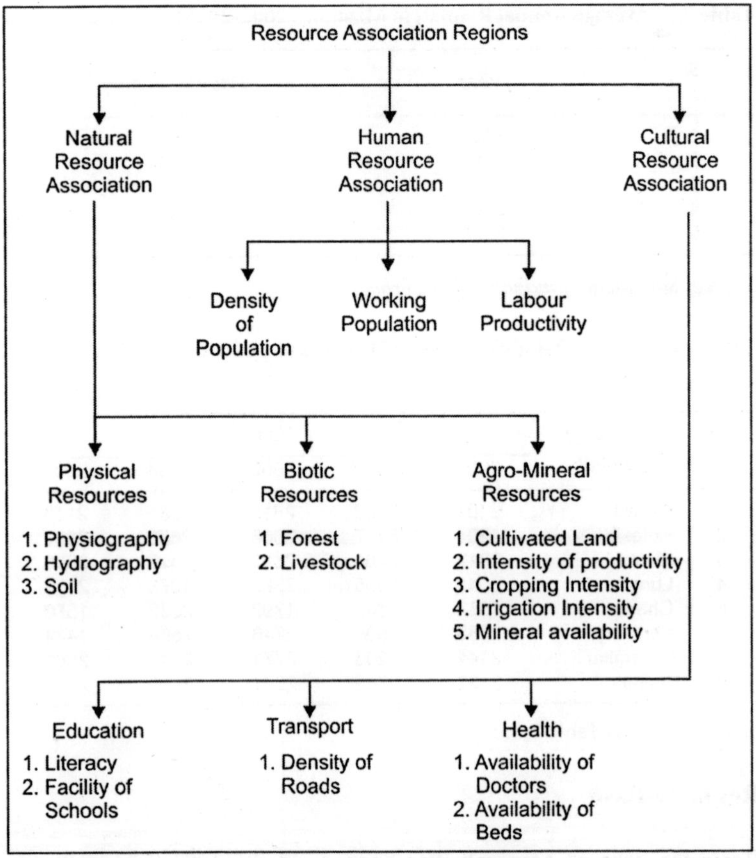

The vegetation of the state is divided into four types based on the nature of forests, viz., tropical, wet evergreen and semi evergreen, montane subtropical, and bamboo forests.

The most important floral group in Mizoram is bamboo, which along with other plantains, grows at the lower altitude of the forest. At higher altitude the woods get denser with canes and creepers. Of the wide variety of floral species the most common are Teak, Sal, Gamari, Duabanga, Chalmugra, Champa, Bel, Jungle neem, Jackfruit, Pine, Mulberry, Oak and Banyan. The floristic diversity as recorded by the Botanical Survey of India (BSI) (1999) comprises 2,141 species of flowering plants (angiosperms-monocot, dicot), 6 species of gymnosperms and 211 species of pteridophytes.

Table 2.5 : Resources in Mizoram by Blocks

(*in Percentages*)

Name of Blocks	Proportion of Natural Resources			Proportion of Human Resources			Proportion of Cultural Resources		
	Physical Resources	Biotic Resources	Agro-mineral Resources	Density of Population	Working Population	Labour Productivity	Education Resources	Transport Resources	Health Resources
1. Tlangnuam	28.9	31.5	39.6	38.8	25.2	35.9	17.9	42.9	39.2
2. Thingdawl	47.6	2.3	50.1	5.2	46.8	48.1	45.0	10.0	25.0
3. Lungdar 'E'	50.7	9.9	40.8	3.5	31.6	65.0	41.2	3.0	55.9
4. Khawzawl	33.3	24.7	42.0	8.5	39.4	52.2	44.9	10.3	44.8
5. Serchhip	44.7	48.7	10.6	42.3	5.6	52.2	50.6	12.7	36.7
6. Thingsulthliah	29.7	31.1	35.2	33.7	29.7	36.6	34.4	12.5	53.1
7. Ngopa	47.7	27.3	25.0	45.0	25.0	30.0	33.3	41.7	25.0
8. Aibawk	13.5	62.7	33.8	44.8	13.8	41.4	29.7	50.0	20.3
9. Darlawn	35.2	35.3	29.5	31.4	34.2	34.3	36.5	47.6	15.9
10. W.Phaileng	40.8	5.9	50.8	27.0	26.9	46.2	45.8	48.8	8.4
11. Zawlnuam	10.9	32.7	56.4	38.0	12.5	50.0	42.4	48.3	19.3
12. Reiek	8.0	68.0	24.0	30.3	33.3	36.4	52.3	36.9	19.8
13. Lunglei	30.4	30.4	39.2	51.2	19.5	29.3	26.8	37.5	35.7
14. Hnahthial	22.2	44.4	33.4	71.8	5.1	23.2	23.2	34.4	42.4
15. Lungsen	27.7	27.7	44.6	44.8	44.7	10.6	9.7	83.9	6.5
16. Bunghmun	50.0	46.9	3.1	55.9	23.3	21.0	13.0	39.1	47.8
17. Tuipang	3.4	27.5	69.0	23.9	62.7	13.4	23.4	25.0	51.6
18. Sangau	33.3	38.9	27.8	15.7	66.7	17.7	28.0	47.1	25.0
19. Lawngtlai	38.5	51.3	10.2	60.4	22.6	17.0	16.0	44.0	40.0
20. Chawngte	44.7	49.4	5.9	19.7	65.6	14.8	25.0	45.5	29.5

Source: Kumar, G. (2003), *Resource Association Regions-Quest for a Development Strategy – A Case Study of Mizoram* in "Modernisation of the Mizo Soceiety" (ed.), R.N. Prasad and A.K. Agarwal, Mittal Publications, New Delhi.

Table 2.6: Percentage Contribution by Each Type of Resources

Name of Blocks	*Proportion of Resources*		
	Natural Resources	*Human Resources*	*Cultural Resources*
1. Tlangnuam	25.49	41.17	33.34
2. Thingdawl	37.25	33.33	29.42
3. Lungdar 'E'	35.37	25.00	39.63
4. Khawzawl	45.57	34.17	20.36
5. Serchhip	36.78	31.07	32.19
6. Thingsulthliah	39.47	52.63	7.90
7. Ngopa	38.18	29.09	32.73
8. Aibawk	21.54	46.15	32.31
9. Darlawn	4.54	54.54	40.92
10. W.Phaileng	31.25	18.75	50.00
11. Zawlnuam	28.57	17.14	54.29
12. Reiek	15.38	38.46	46.16
13. Lunglei	7.14	42.86	50.00
14. Hnahthial	38.80	2.98	58.22
15. Lungsen	8.69	82.61	8.70
16. Bunghmun	54.83	12.90	32.27
17. Tuipang	21.82	40.00	39.18
18. Sangau	55.32	19.15	25.53
19. Lawngtlai	54.83	22.58	22.59
20. Chawngte	60.60	27.22	12.13

Source: Same as Table 2.1.

As to the faunal resource of Mizoram, a recent survey by the scientists of the Zoological Survey of India (ZSI) focuses on nearly 1,468 species belonging to 891 genera under 295 families, of which insects alone form 37 per cent with 520 species; the next abundant group is the birds with nearly 370 species and sub-species distributed in the State. To name the important species of mammals found in the deep forests of Mizoram are Tigers, Elephants, Malayan Sun Bears, Himalayan Black Bears, Small toothed Civet, Clawless Otter, Serow, Hoolock Gibbon, Monkey, Capped Langur, Brush tailed Porkupines, Mangoose and Barking Deer. The bird population of Mizoram belongs to the rare species, such as Hornbills, Pea-pheasants, Lower peckers, Large hawks, Cuckoos, Craw-pheasants and forest Eagle. However, the important birds found in the state are Owl, Pheasants, Partridge, Hawk, Eagle, Egret, Myna, Bulbul, Heron and Cuckoo.

Socio-Cultural Background

It is extremely difficult to draw any boundary between culture, religion and customs of any tribe as they are inseparably intertwined. Like any other tribe, the Mizos were nomadic tribes wandering from place to place. A brief account of the different aspects of Mizo society is given below.

Ethnicity

Historically, the people of Mizoram came from the so-called Sinlung located on the banks of the Yalung River in China, and, therefore, Mongoloid in origin, similar to that of many tribes of the northeastern Indian states (ERCM Report, 2009). The earliest Mizos who migrated to India were known as Kukis, the second batch of immigrants was called New Kukis. The Lushais were the last of the Mizo tribes who migrated to India. The Mizos are divided into numerous sub-tribes— The Lushai, Hmar, Ralte, Paihte, Mara, Lai, etc.

About 87 per cent of the population of Mizoram is Christian; a majority of them are Protestants. There are also Buddhist (8%), Hindu (3.5%), and Muslim (1%) minorities. The nomadic Chakmas practice a combination of Hinduism, Buddhism, and Animism.

Festivals and Dances

Festivals and dances of the Mizos have a unique tribal flavour. As Christians, Christmas and the New Year's Day are celebrated as the most popular occasions. Chapchar Kut (in March), Pawi Kut (in December) and Mim Kut (in September) were also important festivals in the past which are still celebrated with popular community programmes. Among the Chakmas the important cultural festivals are Biju (in April), Alpalani (in July) etc. The most popular dances of Mizoram are *Cheraw* (Bamboo dance), *Khuallam* (dance for visitors or guests), *Chheih Lam* and *Solakia* or *Sarlamkai* (prevalent among the *Mara* and *Pawi* tribes).

Language

In Mizoram the main language is Mizo. However, English is another important language in the state which is understood by majority of the people. In the State Government offices both English and Mizo are almost equally used. In southern Mizoram Lakher, Lai and Chakma languages are being spoken by the micro-minority tribes.

The present Mizo language belongs to the Indo-Tibetan language group spoken by about 6,000 people as given in the first Census, 1901. In the language spoken by different tribes, there are dialectical differences, but they could, to some extent, be understood by the different tribes. At the close of the 19th century, when the British missionaries arrived in Lushai Hills, the *Duhlian* dialect was mainly used by the *Sailo* Chiefs and their subjects. The missionaries picked up the *Duhlian* dialect and created Mizo alphabets based on Roman scripts.

Community Life

Historically, the Mizo society was based largely around tribal villages. The Chief, in consultation with a group of *Upas* (elders), ran the administration of the village. Although each village maintained its own autonomy, there was a net of the ruling clans like the *Sailo*, the *Zadeng*, the *Fanai, the Chenkual,* etc. The British did not attempt to bring about any radical change in the village administration; instead they made use of the existing system for their governance. It was with the Independence of India that radical changes in the system of governance were brought about by doing away with 'Chieftainship' and replacing it by the system of Village Council in Mizoram.

The Institution of 'Zawlbuk'

Zawlbuk (Bachelor's Quarters) is a unique institution of the early Mizo society. It was usually constructed by the voluntary labour of the village community, generally in the heart of the village, near the Chief's house. In the *Zawlbuk,* all the young men slept at night. In some big villages, each locality, usually inhabited by the people of the same clan, had a separate *Zawlbuk.* The *Val upa* (senior bachelors) were responsible for the administration of *Zawlbuk* to arrange for all works to be done by the inmates in the event of war, death, protection of wild animals and accidents of the villagers.

The *Zawlbuks* were of strategic importance to the village community. It performed a wide range of functions among which the most important ones are—(i) protection of the village; (ii) training young people; (iii) discussing common issues; and (iv) recreation and fellowship. In fact, *Zawlbuk* served as an important means of organized community life. The basic tenet which governed the *Zawlbuk* was the principle of *Tlawmngaihna,* which literally means resistance to seeking help from others, instead the focus is on helping others who are in need. *Tlawmngaihna* embraces various types of human qualities and activities, and manifests itself in various forms and aspects of community life which can be summed up as "community over self." The *Zawlbuk* was essentially a training institute for young men and boys to learn the art of wrestling, singing, dancing, oratory, handicrafts and technique of war; for instruction about sex, manners, traditions, customs and etiquette. Thus, it qualifies to be the institution of informal education in those days.

Political History

As to the political history of Mizoram, very little is known. The Mizo (formerly known as *Lushai*) tribes migrated from the nearby Chin Hills between 1750 and 1850 and subjugated the indigenous population. The similar tribes got assimilated into their own society. Based on hereditary 'Chieftainhood' the Mizos developed an autocratic political system.

The socio-political system of the Mizos was not affected by foreign political influence until the British annexed Assam in 1826 under the Treaty of Yandabo. During the next decades, the Mizos raided the British territory of Assam which led to occasional punitive expeditions by the British. Although not formally annexed until the early 1890s, the region had come under the British control two decades earlier. The British divided the Mizo community for their administrative convenience into Burma (now Myanmar) and India; while almost half of the population lived in Myanmar, a larger community lived in India. For the first few years after the British annexation, Lushai hills in the north remained under Assam while the southern half remained under Bengal. Both these parts were amalgamated on 1st April, 1898 into one district called Lushai Hill

District under the Chief Commissioner of Assam (Rosanga, 1990). Under the British administration, the Chiefs used to run the administration. In addition to the collection of paddy by the Village Chief, a land tax of Rs.2 (at that time) was also collected from every house hold. Mizoram was divided into several administrative circles. Each administrative circle was governed by a Circle Inspector.

With the Independence of India, political consciousness developed among the young educated people. Three political options were offered, namely to join either the Indian Union or Burma (Myanmar) or to opt out from either of them and to remain as Crown Colony of the British. The Mizo Union which was formerly known as the Commoner Party against the ruling Chiefs opted for joining the Indian Union whereas the United Mizo Freedom Organization (UFMO) opted for joining Burma. Although the political objective of joining the Indian Union was opting for democracy, democracy did not become a political slogan. The slogan was, in fact, doing away with Tax and Collection of Paddy by the Chiefs. That really appealed to the Mizo People and the Mizo Union consequently became the leading political party.

The country's Independence led to an important landmark for Lushai Hills which was made an autonomous district under the Sixth Schedule to the Constitution of India. A Regional Council (P-L Region) was created in 1953 for the region inhabited by the Pawi, Lakher and Chakma. In 1954, the Lushai Hill District was renamed as Mizo District by an Act of Parliament, viz., Lushai Hills District (Change of Name) Act, 1954.

The growing political consciousness around this time coupled with the distress of the devastating *Mautam* (Bamboo Flowering) famine of 1959 led to the secessionist movement among some Mizos to attain sovereignty. Steadily the movement gained momentum and eventually took up arms on 26th February, 1966 in a bid to achieve its goal. The Mizo Hills was immediately declared a 'Disturbed Area' and security forces were deployed to maintain law and order.

With the implementation of the North-Eastern Areas (Reorganization) Act of 1971, the Mizo District was upgraded into Union Territory and renamed as Mizoram on 21st January, 1972. One of the first administrative moves taken by the Government of the new Union Territory was to divide Mizoram into three districts –

Aizawl, Lunglei and Chhimtuipui with their headquarters at Aizawl, Lunglei and Saiha, respectively. The Pawi-Lakher Region was also trifurcated into Lai, Mara and Chakma Autonomous District Councils.

As a consequence of the signing of the historic Memorandum of Settlement between the Government of India and the Mizo National Front (MNF) in 1986, and by virtue of the passage of the 53rd Constitutional Amendment Bill and the State of Mizoram Bill (1986), Mizoram was granted Statehood on 20th February, 1987 and thus became the 23rd State of the Indian Union.

Administrative Set-up

At present Mizoram has a single-chamber Legislative Assembly of 40 seats. The State sends two members to the Indian Parliament: one to the Rajya Sabha (Upper House) and one to the Lok Sabha (Lower House). The State has eight districts, three Autonomous District Councils, twenty-three Sub-divisions and twenty-two Rural Development Blocks. Table 2.7 shows the districts of Mizoram with their headquarters and sub-divisions.

Aizawl District, the state capital, is having three sub-divisions – Aizawl Sadar, Sakawrdai and Saitual. Saiha, the remotest district bordering Myanmar is having only two sub-divisions, namely Saiha and Tuipang. All other districts have three sub-divisions each including the newly created districts of Mamit, Kolasib, Champhai and Serchhip. Besides having three sub-divisions Lawngtlai district also has two Autonomous District Councils, i.e. Lai and Chakma

Table 2.7: Districts of Mizoram with Headquarters and Sub-Divisions

Sl. No.	*Name of the District*	*Headquarters*	*Sub-divisions*
1.	Aizawl	Aizawl (Sadar)	Aizawl (Sadar), Sakawrdai and Saitual
2.	Champhai	Champhai	Champhai, Khawzawl and Ngopa
3.	Kolasib	Kolasib	Kolasib, Vairengte and Kawnpui
4.	Lawngtlai	Lawngtlai	Lawngtlai, Tuichhak and Chawngte
5.	Lunglei	Lunglei	Lunglei, Hnahthial and Tlabung
6.	Mamit	Mamit	Mamit, Kawrthah and West Phaileng
7.	Saiha	Saiha	Saiha and Tuipang
8.	Serchhip	Serchhip	Serchhip, Vanlaiphai and Thenzawl

Source: *Statistical Handbook of Mizoram*, various issues.

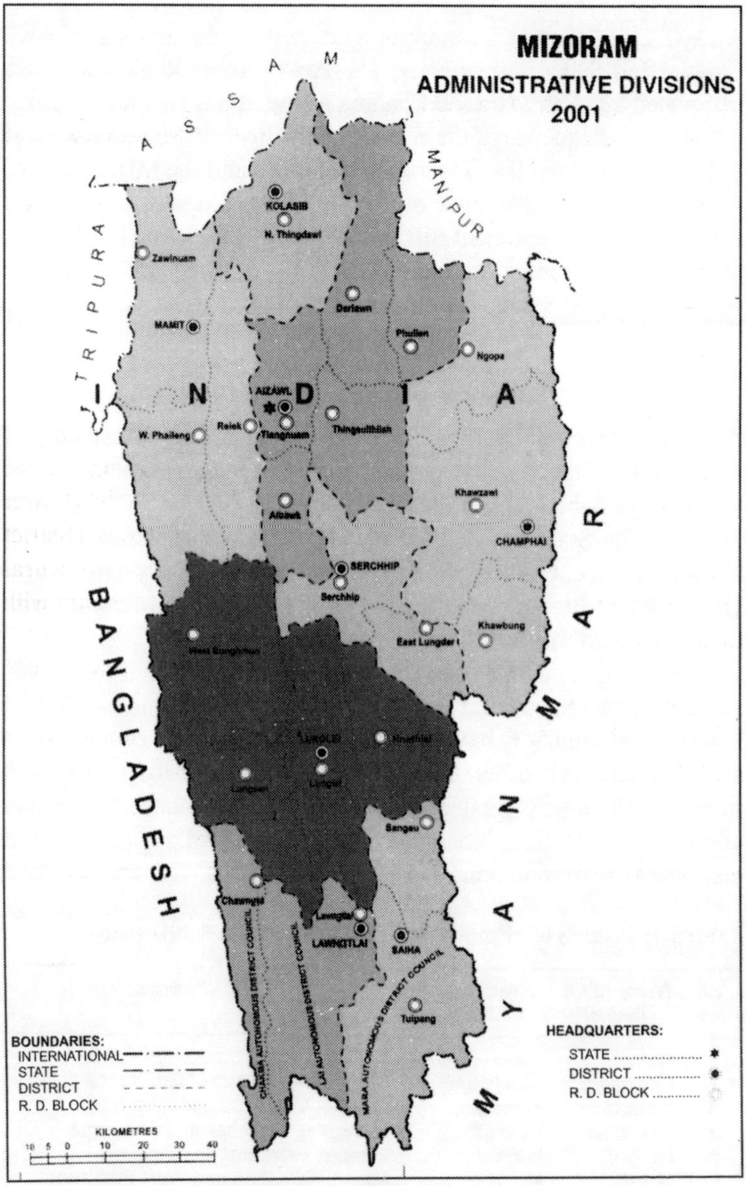

Map 2.2: Mizoram: Administrative division, 2001

Autonomous District Council, while Mara Autonomous District Council falls under the jurisdiction of Saiha district.

Among the eight administrative districts Lunglei is the largest with an area of 4538 square kilometres and four rural development Blocks, while Kolasib district is the smallest with an area of 1382.51 square kilometres. Each district is administered by a Deputy Commissioner, while the Sub-Divisional Officer (Civil) is the administrative head of the sub-division. The Rural Development Blocks in the state are under Block Development Officers.

As stated above, there are three Autonomous District Councils in the state. According to the provision of the Sixth Schedule of the Constitution of India, these District Councils were created to look after their interests and welfare. Table 2.8 presents the area, population and headquarters of the three District Councils of Mizoram.

Table 2.8: Autonomous District Councils with Headquarters, Area and Population (2001)

Sl. No.	*Name of Autonomous District*	*Headquarters*	*Area (in sq. km.)*	*Population (in number)*
1.	Lai	Lawngtlai	1870.75	73620
2.	Mara	Saiha	1399.90	61056
3.	Chakma	Kamalanagar	686.35	34529
Total			**3957.00**	**169205**

Source: *Statistical Handbook of Mizoram,* 2004.

It is seen from Table 2.8 that, Lai Autonomous District Council is the biggest one with an area of 1870.75 square kilometres and a population size of 73620 persons, while Chakma Autonomous District Council happens to be the smallest one measuring an area of 686.35 kilometres and a population of 34529 persons, according to 2001 Census.

The Autonomous Districts Councils are provided with certain powers by the Sixth Schedule of the Constitution of India and have full authority over the management of Primary Education with effect from 1980 and Middle School Education with effect from 1998 within the area of their jurisdiction. However, in actual practice, the Department of Education of the State continues to play significant administrative and academic role in the field of Primary and Middle School Education in the Autonomous District Councils. In fact, all Education Rules and Regulations are made by the State Department of Education and it also exercises control over the final allocation of funds, thus, restricting the powers of the Autonomous District Councils. However, right from secondary level higher education is outside the purview of the District Councils.

Population Profile

According to 2001 Census the Population of Mizoram is 8,88,573. The Scheduled Tribe population in the state was 8,39,310, i.e. 94.45 per cent of the total population of the state. The Scheduled Caste population was only 272. The population consists of 4,59,109 males and 4,29,464 females, by which the sex ratio works out to be 935 females per 1000 males. The density of population as compared to other major states of India is still very low. Stated otherwise, the population is thinly distributed as compared to other states. The density of population in the state as per the latest Census is 42 per square kilometre while that of all India is 324 according to 2001 census.

Decadal Variation

Table 2.9 shows the decadal variation of population in Mizoram during 1901 to 2001. In 1901 the total number of population in Mizoram was only 82,434 persons which increased to 8,88,573 in 2001. This shows that during the last century, the population of Mizoram has increased by 8,06,139 persons, i.e., 978 per cent. On an average, the population of Mizoram has increased by 80,613 persons per decade during the period 1901-2001.

It is seen from Table 2.9 that, the lowest growth rate, i.e. 7.90 per cent was witnessed during 1911-1921 where as the highest growth rate, i.e. 48.55 per cent was registered during 1971-81. However, the decennial growth rate of population during the period 1991 to 2001 was 28.82 per cent, which works out to be around 2.8 per cent per annum which was observed to be lower by 10.87 per cent than the previous decade. The growth rate of population of the state has been higher than the national average in the past decade.

Table 2.9: Decadal Variation of Population in Mizoram (1901-2001)

Sl. No.	Year	Persons	Density (per sq.km)	Males	Females	Decadal variations	% of Decadal variations
1.	1901	82434	4	39004	43430	–	–
2.	1911	91204	4	43028	48176	+8770	10.64
3.	1921	98406	5	46462	51754	+7202	7.90
4.	1931	124404	4	59186	65218	+25998	26.42
5.	1941	152786	7	73855	78931	+28382	22.81
6.	1951	196202	9	96136	100066	+43416	28.42
7.	1961	266063	13	132465	133598	+69861	35.61
8.	1971	332390	16	170824	161566	+66327	24.93
9.	1981	493757	23	257239	236518	+161367	48.55
10.	1991	689756	33	358978	330778	+195999	39.69
11.	2001	888573	42	459109	429464	+198817	28.82

Source: Census of India, 1981. Series–31. Mizoram, Census of India, 1991. Series–17. Mizoram and Census of India, 2001, Series–16. Mizoram.

Districtwise Population

Consequent upon the internal reorganization of the state in 1998, it now has eight districts carved out of the erstwhile three districts. Since the area is hilly, the topography is not much suitable for comfortable and heavy concentration of population in one locality and, also because the traditional system of occupation continues to be the mainstay for a large section of the society, the State has a low density of population. This is equally true of the districts. Table 2.10

Table 2.10: Districtwise Area and Population of Mizoram (2001)

Sl. No.	Name of District	Area (sq/km)	Population	Density (per sq. km.)	Percentage of total population
1.	Aizawl	3576.31	325676	91	36.65
2.	Champhai	3185.83	108392	34	12.20
3.	Kolasib	1382.51	65960	47	7.42
4.	Lawngtlai	2557.10	73620	28	8.29
5.	Lunglei	4538.00	137233	30	15.44
6.	Mamit	3025.75	62785	21	7.07
7.	Saiha	1399.00	61056	43	6.87
8.	Serchhip	1421.60	53861	37	6.06
	Mizoram	**21087.00**	**888573**	**42**	**100**

Source: *Statistical Handbook*, Mizoram, 2004.

shows the districtwise distribution of population with density and area in square kilometres.

The heaviest concentration of population is in Aizawl District, the state capital with a population of 3,25,676 followed by Lunglei and Champhai districts. More than half of the total population of the state (64.29%) lives in these three districts alone. This may be due to the better infrastructural and other civic amenities available in these districts as compared to other parts of the state. Serchhip district with an area of 1421 square kilometre is having a total population of only 53861 persons which shows the lowest concentration of human settlement.

The density of population is highest in Aizawl district which is about 91. Mamit, the newly created district shows the lowest density of population at 21. Lunglei, the largest district in the state has the density of only 30 people, while Kolasib district has 47 persons per square kilometre. The density of population in Saiha, Lawngtlai, Champhai and Serchhip is about 43, 28, 34 and 37, respectively. When compared to the national density of 324 the overall density of population in the state is much below at 42 only.

Occupational Structure

Occupational structure of a population has great economic significance in a country or region. The total number of healthy persons with capabilities to work constitutes the working population of a country. The workers participation rate or the proportion of

Table 2.11: Occupational Structures in Mizoram (2001)

Sl. No.	Category	Number	Percentage
1.	Total population	888573	—
2.	Number of workers (Total workforce)	467159	52.6%
3.	Cultivators	256332	54.9%
4.	Agricultural labourers	26783	5.7%
5.	Household industrial workers	7100	1.5%
6.	Other workers	176944	37.9%

Source: Mizoram at a glance; Directorate of Census Operations, Government of India. Aizawl, Mizoram.

population engaged in economic activities varies from one region to another depending upon several factors like age, sex, life expectancy, definition of worker, wage structure, attitude towards work and availability of work etc. (Zonunthara, 2001).

In Table 2.11 the occupational structure of Mizoram is shown. Out of a total population of 8,88,573 persons there are 4,67,159 number of workers, showing a 56.6 per cent work participation rate in Mizoram. There are few agricultural labourers (5.7%) and more cultivators (54.9%) in the agricultural sector, which constitute the largest proportion of the total workforce. With only 7100 household industrial workers the secondary sector accounts for 1.5 per cent of the total workforce and the rest 37.9 per cent (1,76,944 persons) are other workers.

Economic Scene

The economy of Mizoram is pre-dominantly an agricultural one. Nearly 60.6 per cent of the total workforce is engaged in this sector, while only 1.5 per cent and 37.9 per cent of the working population is engaged in secondary and tertiary sector, respectively. The important economic aspects of Mizoram are discussed in the following section.

State Domestic Product

The single most important indicator to measure the overall economic performance of a state is the estimate of its State Domestic Product (SDP). The State Domestic Product is defined as a measure in monetary terms of the volume of all goods and services produced within the boundaries of the state during a given period, generally one year, accounted without duplication. Table 2.12 provides the detailed estimate of the same.

It is evident from Table 2.12 that, in real terms Gross State Domestic Product (GSDP) at factor cost was ₹ 280891 lakhs in 2009-10 as against ₹ 262033 lakhs in 2008-09. The growth in GSDP during 2009-10, therefore, is recorded at 7.20 per cent as compared to the growth rate of 7.00 per cent in 2008-09 over the previous year.

Table 2.13 furnishes the performance of the different sectors in the economy of Mizoram during 2009-10. The remarkable

Table 2.12: GSDP of Mizoram at Factor Cost by Economic Activity (at Constant 1999-2000 Prices)

(In ₹ Lakhs)

Sl. No.	Industry	2007-08 (P)	2008-09 (Q)	2009-10 (A)
1.	Agriculture, Forestry and Fishing	37983	39066	40328
2.	Mining and Quarrying	1321	1653	2066
3.	Manufacturing	5460	6651	8110
4.	Electricity, Gas and Water Supply	8491	8720	8955
5.	Construction	32041	33643	35325
6.	Trade, Hotels, Transport and Communication	28607	31710	35183
7.	Financing, Insurance, Real Estate and Business Services	55819	61209	67120
8.	Community, Social and Personal Services	75180	79381	83894
	Total	**244902**	**262033**	**280891**

Note: P = Provisional; Q = Quick; and A = Advanced Estimates.
Source: Economic Survey, Mizoram, 2009-10.

contribution of the tertiary or service sector constituting a share of about 67 per cent of the total GDP clearly indicates that this sector drives the economy of Mizoram. Industry or secondary sector contributes about 19 per cent, while agriculture and allied sector contributes the least at 14 per cent of the GDP, although majority of the people are engaged in agricultural activities.

Table 2.13: Sectoral Shares to GSDP (2009-10)

(Percentages)

Sl. No.	Sector	Contribution
1.	Agriculture and Allied	13.78
2.	Industry	18.61
3.	Service	67.61
Total		**100.00**

Source: Same as Table 2.12

Agriculture

In spite of the agrarian characteristics of the economy, the agricultural sector in Mizoram is not much productive. The main system of cultivation is shifting (jhumming) in nature, which is largely because of the unique topography of the state and age-old tradition of the cultivators. Shifting cultivation is economically unproductive, ecologically unsound, and technologically unviable. Being the land of high hills, Mizoram has scarcity of plain and irrigable areas for productive agriculture.

Mizoram has a total land area of 2108700 hectares. Out of the total land, forest covers about 75.58 per cent. The land not available for cultivation constitutes 6.31 per cent and the share of other uncultivated land is 3.19 per cent. Fallow land accounts for 10 per cent, leaving only 4.92 per cent as net sown area (Table 2.14).

Table 2.14: Land Utilisation in Mizoram (2008-09)

Sl. No.	*Area under*	*In '000 hectares*	*% of total*
1.	Forest	1593.700	75.58
2.	Not available for cultivation	133.000	6.31
3.	Other uncultivated land	67.226	3.19
4.	Fallow land	210.939	10.00
5.	Net sown area	103.835	4.92
Total		**2198.700**	**100.00**

Source: Statistical Abstract of Mizoram, 2009

As to the agricultural production, the area and production of some important major crops of Mizoram is shown in Table 2.15. During the five years time, i.e., between 2004-05 and 2008-09, both the area and production of all the principal crops (only five are taken), except for sugarcane, have declined considerably.

The production of sugarcane has marginally increased from 13565 metric tonnes in 2004-05 to 13696 metric tonnes in 2008-09, while the area under cultivation shows a marginal decline from 1357 hectares to 1342 hectares during the same period. The production of paddy has decreased sharply from 107740 metric tonnes in 2005-06 to 42091 metric tonnes in 2006-07 on the onset of 'Mautam' (Bamboo Flowering). For the same reason, the production of oilseeds and sugarcane shows a drastic fall in 2006-07 and 2007-08.

Table 2.15: Area and Production of Major Crops in Mizoram (2004-05 to 2008-09)

Year	*Paddy*		*Maize*		*Pulses*		*Oilseeds*		*Sugarcane*	
	Area (ha.)	*Production (MT)*	*Area (ha.)*	*Production (MT)*	*Area (ha.)*	*Production (MT)*	*Area (ha.)*	*Production (MT)*	*Area (ha.)*	*Production (MT)*
2004-05	57085	107661	10505	19788	6741	7971	5817	5321	1357	13565
2005-06	56460	107740	11742	22703	6861	8663	5870	5560	1383	15953
2006-07	52851	42091	10775	20969	5054	5833	4075	3755	1340	12187
2007-08	54541	15688	7328	729	5048	2632	8485	748	883	828
2008-09	51990	68917	9558	9318	3931	3646	3275	2514	1342	13696

Source: Same as Table 2.14.

Industry

In the absence of large and medium scale industries in the state of Mizoram, the industrial activities are confined to cottage and small scale industries. The entire state has been notified as backward and is categorized as "no industry state". Weaving, bamboo and cane works, woodcarvings, pottery, blacksmithy and handicrafts have been the traditional household industries in Mizoram.

There were 6332 registered small scale industrial units in 2007 in the state. Out of the total, Aizawl district alone accommodates 4911 (77.56%) number of SSI units. Lunglei had only 815 (12.87%), while the remaining 9.57 per cent small scale industrial units were scattered in the rest of the six districts. This is due to the poor infrastructural facilities in the newly created districts.

There are 73 different trades operating in the state of Mizoram which has been classified into 24 groups. The small scale industrial units include food products like bakery and confectionery, pickle making, chow making, chips, ice cream, etc., wood products and furniture, knitting and tailoring, hosiery and garments, handlooms and handicrafts, paper products and printing, steel fabrication, bamboo products, leather and metal products, mini flour mills, computer and related activities, T.V. and electronics repairing units, chemical and chemical products, construction and related activities, truck and bus body building etc., and other miscellaneous manufacturing industries.

Metal products like steel fabrication, grills, shutters, gates, door and window frames, steel furniture, utensils etc., with 1051 units (16.59%) dominates the small scale sector. Wood products like carpentry works, furniture making, and mini saw mills etc., accounts for 13.75 per cent (871 units) in the state. Industrial units related to wood products are scattered all over the state. This is mainly due to the availability of plenty of forest resources in the state (Laskar, 2010).

Infrastructure

The overall economic development of a country or a region depends on the level of infrastructural facilities it possesses. Infrastructural facilities may be defined as the capital of a society that is embodied in such forms as it helps direct productive activities (Agarwal, 1995).

Infrastructure generally consists of transport and communications, power and electricity, water supply, banking and social overheads like education and health.

Table 2.16 lists out the basic indicators of infrastructure in Mizoram in 2008-09. With a total of 5783.31 kilometres road length per 1000 population stands at 6.51 kilometres in the state. The number of motor vehicles per 1000 population is calculated to be 77.80 in

Table 2.16 : Basic Indicators of Infrastructure in Mizoram (2008-09)

Sl. No.	*Particulars*	*Units*
1	Transport and communications	
	Total road length	5783.31 kms.
	National Highway	886.00 kms.
	State Highway	698.94 kms.
	Length of Railway network	.5 kms.
	Total Motor Vehicles	69130 Nos.
	Airport	1 No.
2	Electricity and Water Supply	
	Installed capacity	40.77 M.W.
	Villages electrified	570 Nos.
	Per capita power consumption	186.23 KWH
	Habitations with water supply	526 Nos.
3	Finance and Banking	
	Banks/Branches	109 Nos.
	Total Deposits (In ₹ crores)	1914.83
	Total Advance (In ₹ crores)	1158.99
	Credit Deposit Ratio (%)	60.53
4	Health and Education	
	Hospitals	12 Nos.
	Community Health Centres	12 Nos.
	Primary Health Centres	57 Nos.
	Sub-Health Centres	370 Nos.
	Birth rate (per '000)	21.45
	Death rate (per '000)	6.28
	Primary Schools	1783 Nos.
	Middle Schools	1253 Nos.
	High Schools	502 Nos.
	Hr. Sec. Schools	86 Nos.
	Colleges	26 Nos.
	Polytechnics	2 Nos.
	University (including ICFAI)	2 Nos.

Source: 1. *Economic Survey*, Mizoram, 2009-10.
2. *Statistical Abstract of Mizoram*, 2009.

2008-09. The state is connected by metre gauge railway line with a total length of only 1.5 kilometres up to Bairabi. Besides, there is a Railway out agency at Aizawl and a Public Reservation System at Lunglei which provide facilities for computerized railway booking for the people. Mizoram has only one Airport at Lengpui near Aizawl which facilitates regular scheduled flights to and fro from Kolkata, Guwahati and Imphal.

As to the power situation in the state, Mizoram has an installed capacity of 40.77 mega watts (MW) and the per capita consumption was 186.23 KWH during 2008-09. Out of 707 villages 570 are electrified, representing a very satisfactory electrification scenario in the state. Regarding the supply of safe drinking water 526 habitations (out of 777) were covered up to the year 2008-09.

On the front of banking, the state has as many as 109 branches of different (mostly SBI) banks, including the new generation banks like the Axis Bank. The total deposits in the banks was ₹ 1914.83 crores and the total advance was ₹ 1158.99 crores, thus representing a Credit Deposit ratio (CD) of 60.53 per cent during 2008-09.

Among the health indicators mention may be made of 12 Hospitals, 12 Community Health Centres, 57 Primary Health Centres and 370 Sub Health Centres. The birth rate and death rate in the state is 21.45 and 6.28 per 1000 people.

In so far as the infrastructural facility for higher education is concerned, there is a Central University in the state capital and a Campus of the Institute of Chartered Financial Analysts of India (ICFAI) University, established by State legislation. At the undergraduate level, there are 22 general degree colleges, 2 teachers' training colleges, 1 Law college and 1 Veterinary and Animal Husbandry college. There are 2 Polytechnics in the state for providing technical education leading to diploma level.

REFERENCES

Agarwal, A.N. (1995), *Indian Economy: Problems of Development and Planning*, Wiley Eastern Limited, Delhi.

Census of India, (1981), Series-31. Mizoram, Census of India, 1991. Series-17. Mizoram and Census of India, 2001, Series-16. Mizoram.

Economic Survey, Mizoram, 2009-10.

Government of Mizoram (2009), *Education Reform Commission of Mizoram Report, Aizawl* http://www.mizoram.nic/about/physiography.htm

Kumar, G. (2003), Resource Association Regions—Quest for a Development Strategy – A Case Study of Mizoram in "*Modernisation of the Mizo Society*" (ed.), R.N. Prasad and A.K. Agarwal, Mittal Publications, New Delhi.

Laskar, B.I. (2010), *Industrialisation in Mizoram: Problems and Prospects*, New Central Book Agency (P) Ltd., Kolkata.

Mizoram at a glance (2001), Directorate of Census Operations, Government of India Aizawl, Mizoram.

Rosanga, O. (1990), Economic History of Mizoram (1900-1940)', (Unpublished Ph.D. Thesis), Department of History, Delhi University, Delhi.

Statistical Abstract of Mizoram, 2009.

Statistical Handbook of Mizoram, various issues.

Zonunthara, S.R. (2001), 'Working of Public Distribution System in Mizoram', (Unpublished Ph.D. Thesis), Department of Economics, NEHU, Shillong.

3

Review of Literature

Investigation into financing of education has become an important area with the emergence of economics of education in the literature of economics since the early 1960s. In this chapter, an attempt has been made to present a brief summary and findings of the research studies in the field of financing of education that were undertaken by individual researchers, organizations, commissions and committees during the last few years.

Costs of education as a subject of attention of economists may be said to have taken off from the works of John Vaizey (1958) who attempted to analyze the costs of British education in particular and compared it with other countries/institutions. Vaizey drew attention towards public costs and private costs and also towards opportunity cost. He defined educational expenditure as current plus capital expenditure at current prices exclusive of transfer payments such as student grants. Vaizey's calculation showed that the ratio of educational expenditure to National Income at factor cost rose dramatically from 3.4 per cent in 1952 to 5.4 per cent in 1965. Even after deduction of all outlays on non-educational functions which happens to be discharged by schools such as catering, boarding and health services from educational expenditure, the ratio is still over 5 per cent.

Schultz (1963) while assessing the economic value of education measured the factor costs of education where he did not consider the costs of such activities which do not directly contribute to and serve educational purposes. Schultz defined factor cost of education as the sum total of costs paid by the student and his family and the costs paid by others such as state or federal government, voluntary organizations etc. As to the components of total resource costs, Schultz identified the following three heads of expenditure on education: (a) school costs or costs incurred by the society on teachers' salaries, supplies, interest and depreciation on capital; (b) opportunity costs of students, i.e. income foregone during school attendance, and (c) incidental school-related costs incurred by individuals, for example, on the purchase of books and on travel. Private resource costs are classified into direct costs consisting of tuition costs, supplies and additional living expenses, opportunity costs incurred by individuals and incidental school related costs. The total cost of education may be found out by summing up all the costs from societal point of view and all the costs from individual point of view.

Schultz (1961) studied the difference in growth of the stock of education and the stock of reproducible physical capital. The stock of education, embodied in labour force, increased 8.5 times between 1900 and 1956, whereas, the stock of reproducible physical capital rose only 4.5 times, both in 1956 dollar prices. These results of Schultz show the capital elasticity of educational investment to be approximately 1.9. In value terms, stock of education accounted for 22 per cent of the stock of physical capital in 1900. The stock of human capital rose to approximately 42 per cent of the total stock of physical capital in 1956 due to more rapid growth of educational investment than the growth of investment in physical investment.

Schultz (1960) also estimated that, income foregone by students constituted more than half of the costs of higher education in the United States of America. Cost of education including foregone earnings, measured by Schultz in terms of current dollar prices increased from 400 million dollar in 1900 to 28.7 billion dollar in 1956. In 1900 income foregone accounted for about one-fourth of the total costs of elementary, secondary and higher education. By 1956 it represented over two-fifths of all costs. The percentage increase in the real costs of education was estimated to be 3.5 times as large as consumer income, suggesting an income elasticity of educational expenditure of 3.5. In dollar terms, educational costs also rose about three and half times as rapidly as did the gross capital formation of physical capital. As for the resource cost per student per annum was estimated to be 280 dollar for elementary, 1420 dollar for high school and 3300 dollar for higher education in 1956. Income foregone constituted 60 per cent and 59 per cent of the total resource cost in case of high school and higher education respectively.

Vaizey and Sheehan (1968) examined the effect of changes in price levels on educational expenditure in Britain for the period 1920-65. In this study, separate price indices for each input in the educational system were calculated. They pointed out that there were changes in the value of real resources devoted to education as well as changes in the cost structure. For example, the fall in teachers' salaries from 70 per cent of all expenditure in 1921 to less than 50 per cent in 1950 is an indication of the above observation.

Hallak (1969) based his study on the experience of France and Tanzania in testing the financial feasibility of educational plans. He decomposed educational cost into public, private and opportunity costs. Two important aspects of his analysis of cost are: (a) to ascertain the place of education in the national economic context, and (b) to define total and unit costs by type and level of education and by purpose of expenditure. Hallak also classified the total educational costs into recurring expenditure, capital expenditure and debt services. In recurring expenditure he includes salaries and allowances of teaching and non-teaching staff, text books, other instructional material expenses and supplies, etc. He also included expenditures on scholarships and grants, welfare services, canteen, transport, boarding, sports, maintenance of buildings and equipments and operations of buildings, like fuel, light, water and gas in this category. Expenditures on purchase and development of land, school buildings, classrooms, laboratories and fixed equipment and welfare services, residence halls etc. come under capital expenditure. Other important estimates like cost per graduate, cost by level of education attained, unit cost per pupil, cost per average daily attendance, capital cost per place, average cost per class and average recurring cost per teacher are showed in this study.

Coombs and Hallak (1972) undertook the analysis of educational costs. The study was based largely on the American system of education and compared it with many developed and developing countries. The major objectives of the study were to have cost analysis for assessing the feasibility of educational projects, to know the cost and consequences of introduction of educational reforms, to draw up a programme of expenditure over planning period and facilitate decision making when several alternative possibilities exist for the allocation of funds. They identified the elements of educational system as– (i) objectives, (ii) outputs, (iii) benefits, (iv) internal process, and (v) inputs. Within the framework of 'system analysis' Coombs and Hallak developed the following ways of measuring and expressing educational costs:

(i) Resource cost *vs*. Money cost,
(ii) Capital cost *vs*. Recurrent cost,
(iii) Unit cost per student, and
(iv) Factor costs of education.

Then they classified the factors affecting educational costs into– (a) external cost determinants, that lie outside the educational system, and (b) internal cost determinants, which are closely allied to the technology adopted by the educational institutions and to the policy employed regarding the payment, deployment and utilization of teachers.

Coombs and Hallak observed that a substantial part of the impressive rise in educational expenditure between the period 1950 and 1970 was not 'real' but was caused by inflation of prices and wages and explosive increase in demand for education.

The main findings of their study were that, educational costs vary not only from one country to another but within one country, from one system to another, and also within different educational systems. Unit cost of education also showed a rising trend in the long run. Besides, unit costs increased with each successive educational level and scientific and technical education at any level is costlier than general education. They found that cost per unit could be reduced by raising the enrolment to an optimal size. But this optimal size of enrolment will be different for different levels of education.

James Maynard (1971) undertook a study of cost of higher education in the USA. He observed that– (a) long run cost function of institutions of higher learning was traditionally U-shaped, (b) parabola was superior to a linear function for explaining variation in per student costs in higher education, (c) per student cost declined over the range of 500 to 5363 for Full Time Equivalence students, and (d) the size of the institutions was a dominant variable in explaining variations in cost per student among similar (of same level) students.

Bottomly (1972), under the auspices of Organization for Economic Co-operation and Development, conducted a study of Bradford University. In this study he calculated economic, capital and teaching costs by departments and courses and arrived at the conclusion that increase in class size reduced the cost per student. He also found that– (a) the total economic cost per student varied between 2500 dollar and 4000 dollar for laboratory based course and for class room based course between 1650 dollar and 2400 dollar, (b) an increase in enrolment can lead to substantial economies in staff costs per student, (c) economies could also be gained by increasing the teaching load on the staff by intensive and extensive use of teaching, accommodation, building and other technical and administrative staff, (d) an increase in enrolment to an optimum level together with a 50 per cent increase in teaching load would reduce the full academic staff cost per student by 46 per cent to 65 per cent of the total cost, and (e) in almost all the courses total economic cost per student can be decreased by 5 per cent to 13 per cent.

Blaug and Woodhall (1967) conducted a study of secondary school costs in the United Kingdom. They observed, in terms of constant prices that, between 1950-51 and 1963-64, per administrative staff and maintenance costs rose by 46 per cent, equipment and furniture costs by 35 per cent, building costs by 35 per cent and per student teacher costs by only 27 per cent.

Macklup (1962) studied the cost of all types of education in the U.S. economy including– (i) education in the home, i.e., earnings foregone by mothers staying at home to educate their pre-school children, (ii) on-the-job training, (iii) education in the church, (iv) education in the Armed Services, and (v) cost of formal education, special schools and other federal expenditure. He concluded that, education is one of the constituents of knowledge industry and the total cost of knowledge production in the United States was 29 per cent of GNP in 1958. Macklup estimated the total cost of education industry at $ 60,000 million which is 14 per cent of GNP while formal education accounted for $ 46,000 million.

Blaug *et al.*, (1969) using the data of the Education Commission (1964-76), the Institute of Applied Manpower Research (IAMR) studies and the official educational statistics, conducted a study of costs of education in India for the year 1960-61 and 1965-66. Two important costs estimated by them were social cost and private cost. The former consists of all current expenditures on educational institutions, costs of inspection, the imputed rented value of educational capital and private expenditure on books and earnings foregone, while the latter comprises fees minus scholarship as well as private expenditure on books and earnings foregone. The imputed rent per pupil on educational capital was estimated by calculating the current replacement cost of all buildings and equipment and amortizing at a constant rate of interest. The average length of life was assumed to be forty years and the earnings foregone during education were directly estimated from the earning profiles available in India.

One of the important findings of their study is, that the earning foregone of even six years old had some significance as they helped to explain the high dropout rates in the early years of primary school. Four important estimates provided by the study were: (i) social costs of educating successful candidates; (ii) social cost of education assuming average levels of wastage and stagnation; (iii) private costs of educating successful students; and (iv) private costs of education assuming average levels of wastage and stagnation. These were done in order to calculate rates of return on investment in education.

Based on twenty-seven case studies, a research project was undertaken by the International Institute for Educational Planning (IIEP) (1972), which concluded that cost analysis could serve the following purposes in educational planning:

(i) Costing and testing the economic feasibility of educational plans;
(ii) Evaluating and improving the allocation of available educational resources;
(iii) Comparing alternative ways of achieving the same objective in order to select the most efficient or economical one;
(iv) Determining both the short-run and long-run cost implications of a particular project;

(v) Estimating the cost of alternative policies and educational reforms and innovations;
(vi) Improving the efficiency of resource utilization; and
(vii) Checking the economic implications and feasibility of special policy decisions before they are made.

Psacharopoulos (1972) made a comparison of the ratio of total costs per student per year by education level for a group of developed and developing countries in his study of returns to education. He found that in the developed countries (viz. USA Great Britain and New Zealand) the ratio of total per pupil costs of secondary to primary education was 6.6 to 1 and that of higher to primary education was 17.6 to 1 while in less developed countries (viz. Malaysia, Ghana, South Korea, Kenya, Uganda, Nigeria and India) these ratio were 11.9 and 87.9 to 1 respectively. It implies, taking the 87.9 to 1 ratio, for the equivalent cost of educating one university student for a year 88 primary school children could have a year of schooling. In many African countries (viz. Sierra Leone, Malawi, Kenya and Tanzania) cost ratio per pupil between higher and primary education ranged as high as 283 to 1.

Becker (1975) while studying the rate of return to investment in college and high school education classified the total cost of education into:

(i) Private costs, which include direct expenditure on tuition fees, books and supplies, travel between home and school, and capital used by students in school works and foregone earnings of the students; and
(ii) Social cost, comprising current educational expenditure, capital used on education, property taxes if schools were not tax-exempted and social opportunity cost.

Becker estimated the average outlay on books and supplies etc., on the basis of the survey conducted by the US Department of Health Education and Welfare in 1952-53. The earnings foregone of the students is estimated by assuming that college students earned about one quarter of the amount earned by high school graduates of the same age and that high school students earned one quarter of the estimated earnings of the elementary school graduates of the age 14 to 17. Current educational expenditure is estimated by subtracting non-educational expenditures from total educational expenditures.

Important findings of the study were that– (a) the tuition payments were 112 dollar per student in 1939 and 242 dollar per student in 1958. Books and supplies consist of 22.5 per cent of tuition, travel 23.9 per cent and capital 7 per cent; and (b) the value of property tax foregone was estimated to be 18 dollar and 21 dollar per student in 1939 and 1949, respectively.

The OECD study group (1977) conducted a cross-section study to estimate the total resource cost of regular education in France, Japan and Great Britain for the year 1970. The study group classified educational costs into the following four categories of expenditure:

(i) Expenditure on personnel which includes salaries and wages of teaching and supporting teaching staff; other emoluments of teaching staff; salaries and wages of non-teaching staff; administration and ancillary staff directly concerned with educational activities, maintenance and welfare payments to staff and students.

(ii) Other current expenditure consisting of maintenance and repair of land and buildings, furniture and equipments, expenditure on replaceable equipments and materials like fuel, water light, heat, cleaning and administrative expenditure other than personal expenses etc.

(iii) Associated expenditure comprising items, like transportation, clothing, catering and boarding expenditure, transfer payments and welfare expenditure.

(iv) Imputed cost which covers the rent of educational buildings and equipment and the earnings foregone by students.

According to this study, the total resource costs of regular education were $9,607 million, $11,667 million and $ 6,829 million for France, Japan and Great Britain, respectively. The share of total resource cost of education as a proportion of Gross National Product (GNP) in France was 6.7 per cent and that of Japan and Great Britain were 5.7 and 5.5 per cent, respectively. Total current expenditure accounted for 49.38 per cent of the total resource cost of education in France while the figure for Japan and Great Britain were 54.02 and 65.79 per cent, respectively. The shares of imputed rent as a proportion of total resource cost were 5.04, 6.76 and 5.15 per cent, respectively for France, Japan and Great Britain. Earning foregone was estimated at 45.58 per cent of the resource cost in France, 39.21 per cent in Japan and 29.05 per cent in Great Britain.

Panchamukhi (1965) studied the total cost of University and Professional education in India for the period 1950-51 to 1959-60. The total expenditure was divided into three categories—expenditure on formal education or education in schools and colleges, expenditure on the job and expenditure in the armed forces. The estimates of cost of formal education included teaching and non-teaching staff salaries, expenditure on equipments and chemicals, library, sports and indirect expenditures like inspection, direction, building, furniture, scholarship, books, transport and other stationeries. To arrive at the total cost, he also calculated the costs of on the job training and training in the armed forces. Panchamukhi found that physical investment in India have been increasing at a higher rate of 13.4 per cent per annum as compared with educational investments. The other finding of his study was that, India had invested nearly 5 to 6 per cent of her national income in education, which was less than half of the U.S. figure at 11.8 and 12.9 per cent of GNP in 1956 and 1958, respectively. In another place Panchamukhi estimated that, over three-fifths of the total educational costs (about ₹ 700 crores) were mainly the earnings foregone by the students.

Shah (1969) studied the private cost of education. He divided private cost into tuition costs and non-tuition costs. He also divided the parents into high income and low income groups in his analysis. Shah observed that, non-tuition costs constitute an important element of private cost of education and students' fees were not considered as a burden by the relatively affluent parents. Items of non-tuition cost were identified as books, stationery, private tuition, transport and refreshment. Private tuition constituted the main item, accounting for 61 per cent of the non-tuition cost for the students of high income families. On the contrary, for the students belonging to low income groups the main items of expenditure were books and stationary, accounting for 85 per cent of the total non-tuition costs.

The trends in investment expenditure in Professional education during the first two Five Year Plans were studied by Shah (1969) in another paper 'Expenditure on Professional School Education in India'. He found that, during the decade 1950-51 to 1960-61, educational expenditure at constant prices increased only by 131.4 per cent as against 209.2 per cent at current prices and expenditure per pupil in professional schools increased by 8.2 per cent in constant prices and 44.6 per cent in current prices.

Institute of Applied Manpower Research (IAMR) in a survey of costs of engineering colleges and polytechnics (1964) observed considerable variations in per pupil cost among Indian Institute of Technology (IITs), Regional Engineering Colleges (RECs) and all other colleges of engineering and technology. For IITs current expenditure per pupil averaged ₹ 2263 per annum, while it was ₹ 1200 and ₹ 483 for RECs and other colleges, respectively. The current expenditure per pupil averaged ₹ 372 per annum. The size-cost relationship with regard to the cost of education of the IIT students at the undergraduate and the post-graduate level was studied by IAMR in 1975. Returns to scale were also measured in terms of cost-elasticity. The study found that:

(a) Optimal enrolment in almost all cases were higher than the actual enrolments;
(b) Fixed costs are higher at the under-graduate level than at the post-graduate level; and
(c) Economies of scale for both under-graduate and post-graduate courses are reaped in case of linear average cost curves.

The Education Commission (1964-66) in a separate study observed a wide variation in the unit costs of higher education in India. These variations were: (i) due to differences in the methodology and scope of the studies, and (ii) due to the differences in the level of facilities and services provided in the institutions. Capital cost plus recurring costs on salaries of teachers, student-teacher ratio, library, laboratory etc., determine the level of facilities and services in the institutions. The Commission found that unit costs in arts and science faculties at the under-graduate are similar.

Dey (1969) classified educational costs into—(a) direct expenditure, (b) expenditure for meals and tiffins, (c) expenditure of students on health service, and (d) expenditure on training of teachers. In the year 1963 a pilot enquiry of public health and educational services in Madhyagram, an urbanized village in the district of 24 Parganas, West Bengal was conducted by B. Dey to collect data for empirical content of his cost classification. The results were that, (i) the direct cost was estimated at ₹ 92.98 per student in the sample secondary schools and (ii) per student total annual cost were calculated at ₹ 106.86 excluding guardian's share of books, stationery, meals and cost of administration and inspection.

Datt (1969) undertook a study of unit cost of college education in Haryana for the year 1965-66. According to him, the important factors affecting the variations of unit cost were – age of the college, enrolment, average pay of teacher and ratio of non-teacher cost to total costs. Rudder Datt found that the unit cost of education was the highest in the case of state colleges ranging from ₹ 403 to ₹ 424 per student while private women colleges had the lowest unit cost ranging from ₹ 252 to ₹ 268 per student. As for the overall scenario, the unit cost of education ranges from ₹ 311 to ₹ 337 per student in Haryana. In another study, Datt (1988) found that both unit cost and state subsidy were higher in case of conventional education system as compared to distance education system. For the year 1984-85, the average cost per student in conventional colleges was as high as ₹ 3516 while the average fee charged was as low as ₹ 257. The amount of state subsidy was ₹ 3259 per student. It means, state support accounted for 72.7 per cent and fee component comprises 7.3 per cent of the average cost per student. In the case of distance education system, cost per student showed a declining trend as enrolment increased. Another finding in respect of the school of correspondence course is that, fee constituted as high as 42 per cent of the cost of education.

Kulkarni (1969) conducted a study of the cost of commerce colleges in Bombay during the period 1962-63 to 1966-67. He identified the main items of college expenditure as teachers' salaries, furniture and library, rent, scholarships and miscellaneous items. Among these items, teachers' salaries accounted for 40 to 50 per cent of the total cost. He also found that unit cost at current prices increased from ₹ 316 to ₹ 453 during the study period while pupil-teacher ratio went down from 33:1 to 25:1.

Pandit (1972) estimated the total cost of education in India including income foregone at 1960-61 prices. He found that educational expenditure as a proportion of national domestic product has gone up to 7.3 per cent in 1965-66 from a mere 3.4 per cent in 1950-51, while the gross capital formation as a proportion of national domestic product rose from 13.1 to 17.93 per cent during the same period.

Sharma (1980) studied the cost of university system in India in terms of operating and capital cost. Operating cost includes teaching inputs, student services, administration and supporting services and examinations/evaluation. Capital cost includes expenditure on buildings, equipments, library and other items. In this study a comparison has been done between general, professional, affiliating and residential universities. In relation to enrolment economies of scale has also been examined. Operating expenses per student were estimated to be ₹ 3570 and ₹ 833 was the capital expenditure of the universities in 1976-77. Unit cost of education in affiliating universities was higher than that of the residential universities. Optimum enrolment for the universities was calculated to be 3100 students, at which economies of scale also accrues.

Sharma and Mridula (1982) studied the cost of providing graduate education in Hindu College, Delhi during the period 1973-74 to 1976-77. Salaries of teaching and non-teaching staff, cost of library services, cost of student services, laboratory expenses and cost of maintenance and repair were considered to be the components of educational cost. Important findings of the study were:

1. Salary cost of teaching and non-teaching staff constituted 70 to 80 per cent of the total costs. The salary of the teaching staff accounted for nearly two-third of the college budget. Salary of supporting teaching staff constituted 5 to 7 per cent and that of ministerial staff 4 to 5 per cent of the total budget.
2. Almost 10 per cent of the total expenditure was spent on subsidies and about 1 per cent of the total budget was spent on laboratories and science contingencies.
3. Total recurring expenditure varied between ₹ 1615 and ₹ 2248 and non-recurring expenditure between ₹ 216 and ₹ 57 during 1973-76.

The authors also made item-wise cost analysis and found that: (a) the college spent ₹ 1059 to ₹ 1541 per student on salary of teachers, (b) nearly ₹ 32 per student is spent in providing sport facilities, (c) amount spent on fee concession was ₹ 40 and between ₹ 143 and ₹ 192 on scholarships, (d) non-recurring expenditure on buying books and library contingencies ranged between ₹ 22 and ₹ 46 per student and ₹ 31 to ₹ 52 per student was spent on buying apparatus and equipment for science faculties.

Mingat and Tan (1985) carried out a study on the distribution of public expenditure on education. They found that in developing countries, as a whole, 6 per cent of the students pursuing higher education received almost 40 per cent of the total public resources. In Latin America 12 per cent of the student in higher education received 42 per cent and in Africa less than 2 per cent of the university going students received over 35 per cent of the public expenditure on education.

Garg (1982) while analyzing the cost structure of Punjab University and its affiliating colleges found that, recurring expenditure increased by 10.04 per cent and capital expenditure by 1.77 per cent per annum during the period 1952-53 to 1974-75. Using parabolic and cubic equation he found that sixteen teaching departments of the university were undersized where enrolment could be increased and six other departments were oversized where admission could be regulated. Hostel expenses in private colleges (at ₹ 2507) per session were higher than in the government colleges (at ₹ 2212). The level of salaries of staff in private colleges was calculated to be 43.88 per cent of the government colleges which makes the recurring cost of government colleges higher than that of the private colleges.

Tilak (1987) estimated the cost of education in his study on the rate of return to educational investment in Andhra Pradesh. He divided educational costs into institutional cost and private cost. Institutional costs consist of current cost and capital cost. Private costs are investments in education which are made by the pupil and his parents/ guardians or both. The elements of private cost are tuition cost, no-tuition or maintenance cost and earnings foregone. The main finding of his study was that, while institutional cost constituted a relatively small part and foregone earnings formed an important part of the cost of education.

Covering all the States and Union Territories of India, Tilak (1990) made another study of the unit cost of higher education in India. This study was based on 1975-76 data and the unit cost was analyzed under three major heads: (i) salaries of teaching staff, (ii) salaries of other staff, and (iii) expenditure on equipments and other appliances. Unit cost analysis was separately done for general education, professional education and other higher education. The study found wide disparities in the unit cost of education between different States and Union Territories and also between different types of higher education. Another finding of the study is that the student-teacher ratio and average salary of teacher were more important factor in explaining the differences in unit cost than the size of the institution.

Again, Tilak (1993) revealed that the expenditure on higher education in India increased from ₹ 172 million in 1950-51 to ₹ 16.5 billion in 1983-84, registering an annual growth rate of 14.8 per cent in current prices. But, in real terms, expenditure on higher education increased only by 11 times during this period. The share of higher education as percentage of GNP had only marginally increased from 0.19 to 0.89 during the same period. In terms of current prices unit cost of higher education increased 4.3 times, while expenditure per student showed a negative growth rate in real terms.

In another study, Tilak (1994) analyzes the educational investment in Asian countries and showed that public expenditure on education increased 32 times in current prices between 1965 and 1990. The rate of growth of educational investment in Asia is the highest among world regions. As a proportion of GNP, total expenditure on education increased from 3.4 per cent to more than 4 per cent during the 25 years period between 1965 and 1990. Among the Asian countries, the rates of growth in South Asian countries were relatively low.

Chalam (1986) studied the cost, finance and productivity of higher education in Andhra Pradesh on the basis of micro and macro data. He observed that the growth rate of educational expenditure was much higher than the growth rate of State Domestic Product. In the year 1975-76, the proportion of SDP spent on higher education was less than 1 per cent in the state. Out of the total expenditure on higher education, only 28.52 per cent was devoted to professional education. In terms of current prices, expenditure on scholarships and buildings explained 42 per cent of the variation in the indirect expenditure, while in constant prices they explain only 28 per cent of the variation. The elasticity of total expenditure with respect to buildings and scholarships and also to the total indirect expenditure on higher education was less than one.

As to the sources of fund for higher education in Andhra Pradesh, Chalam classified them into: (a) the State and Central Government with their agencies, (b) local bodies, and (c) private contribution like fees, endowments, gifts etc. The elasticity of government funds to the private sources was found to be 1.75 in case of general education and 2.51 in case of overall higher education. While the share of private contribution decreases, the role of government in funding higher education continues to increase.

The study showed that unit cost of higher education in government colleges are less than that of the private colleges. As regards the institutional cost, it was found to be more in science courses than in arts, commerce, law and engineering courses. The salary of the teaching staff is seen to be the dominant component of institutional cost accounting for about 80 per cent of the total cost. The institutional costs of post-graduate courses were calculated to be nearly seven times higher than that of graduate courses.

The private costs of education in all the degree courses were found to be 2 to 3 times higher than the institutional costs. But in the case of University Colleges, the private cost was estimated to be less than the institutional cost. Another finding of the study was that the private cost of students increased progressively with the increase in the parental income.

Shri Prakash (1977) in his work "Educational System of India" revealed that the total average unit cost of all levels and types of education taken together increased from ₹ 50 in 1951 to ₹ 67 in 1964, measured at constant 1960-61 prices, indicating a growth rate of 34 per cent. The average direct cost went up from ₹ 40 to ₹ 52, during the same period, representing a growth rate of 30 per cent. A comparison of unit costs of different institutions revealed that, while unit cost per student per year increased from primary to middle and from middle to high/higher secondary schools, the unit cost per student in colleges for general education were higher than that of the universities.

In another study, Prakash (1996) observed the following characteristics of unit cost of education in India: (a) that there is inverse relationship between unit cost and enrolment, (b) that there is direct relationship between costs, quality of education service and number and nature of courses serviced, (c) that the salary cost dominates the recurring cost and recurring cost dominates the unit cost of education, and (d) that the overall and item-wise unit costs are approximated by U-shaped curves. Regarding unit cost of college education in Punjab, Prakash found that cost of specialized instruction in education, science and commerce far exceeded the unit cost of arts and humanities courses. Education in science at the college level was found to be the costliest. Another finding of the study was that, educational cost per unit was higher in public than in private sector.

Prakash and Choudhury (1994) in their study on the structure and growth of public expenditure on education in India during 1951 to 1987 made the following important observations:

(i) Educational expenditure increases as the educational system moves from lower to higher stages of development and educational expenditure grows more rapidly than general expenditure and income.
(ii) Public and private expenditure on education, both in nominal and real terms, increased more rapidly than population, enrolment and real and nominal Net National Product.
(iii) Educational deflators rise more rapidly than general price deflator.
(iv) Income is the significant determinant of expenditure on education and education is found to be a superior good both at social and private level.
(v) Education production function operates under increasing returns to scale. Total educational cost curve approximates second degree parabola and the average cost curve is U-shaped.

Graham (1987) studied the public and private cost of education at the international level. The main findings of the study were as follows: For the world as a whole, per capita public expenditure in 1978 was US $146, which is 5.6 per cent of the world gross national product. The developed nations of Europe and America spend significantly more than the developing nations of Asia and Africa. Per capita public spending in developed countries were US $366, while it was as low as US $26 in developing countries. As a per cent of GNP, Sweden spent the most, per capita, while Haiti spent the least. Among the selected OECD nations, per capita spending was found to be the highest at 139 dollar in Canada and the least at 9 dollar in Italy, the Netherlands and Sweden. Among the European nations, Spain and the United Kingdom recorded the highest private consumption on education. Again, Canadian consumers devoted the largest fraction of their budget to education and Swedish consumers the least.

Agarwal (1988) studied the unit cost of entrepreneurship training programme under conventional and distance mode. For the cost of regular classroom training programme, the case of Small Industry Service Institute (SISI), Karnal, Haryana, and for that of the correspondence service, All India Manufacturers' Organization (AIMO), New Delhi, were studied by Agarwal. It was calculated that the unit cost at AIMO was higher than that of SISI by 39 per cent. A difference in capacity utilization was reckoned to be the main factor responsible for this variation.

Sharma (1993) in his study of Government College, Daman and Navyug Science College, Surat found that unit cost per student in Government College was 2.71times higher in comparison with private college. This was due to (i) lower student-teacher ratio, (ii) small size of enrolment, and (iii) higher average salary of teachers. It was also found that the quantity and quality of academic infrastructure in these non-viable colleges were very poor. Almost all the funds available with these colleges were spent on the salary of teaching and non-teaching staff and a very small amount was left for library, laboratories and other teaching aids. Sharma also estimated the unit cost and effective cost of producing a graduate student at ₹ 40,829 and ₹ 66,880, respectively, for government college, while the amounts were ₹ 15,835 and ₹ 19,341, respectively, for private college.

In a study of the primary education in Mizoram during the post-Independence period, Lalliani (1990) analyzed the growth of enrolment, expenditure and other infrastructural facilities. The study found that the share of public expenditure on primary education increased from 34.5 per cent in 1953-54 to 50.7 per cent in 1971-72, and then it started falling down gradually, reaching 32.2 per cent in 1985-86. The ratio of plan outlay on primary education to total educational outlay has fallen from 36 per cent in the Fifth Plan (1975-80) to a low of only 12 per cent in the Seventh Plan (1985-90), showing a fast declining trend. Item-wise analysis shows that, the proportion of expenditure on teachers' salaries increased from 79.5 per cent in1977-78 to 95.7 per cent in 1982-83. In the year 1986-87 the annual non-teacher cost per pupil was calculated to be ₹ 75, while the costs of physical formation like buildings, etc., constituted only 1 per cent of the total outlay, indicating inadequate infrastructural facilities at the primary level of education in Mizoram.

Mathew (1991) studied the sources and uses of funds of private colleges in Kerala. In this exercise both institutional and non-institutional sources of finance were examined. Among the institutional sources of finances, state government grants constitute over 90 per cent. A major share of the total grant, however, is earmarked for payment of salaries of the teachers, who are highly organized, and grants allotted for the provision of such basic facilities as libraries and laboratories which directly contribute to the academic performance of colleges are ridiculously meagre. Of the non-institutional sources of finance, donations are by far the most important. Several colleges try to overcome the inadequacy of government grants by resorting to compulsory donations. The study has brought out the fact that the practices of accepting or not accepting donations as a precondition for appointment of teachers and/or admission of students does not by itself lower or raise the quality of higher education. Mathew, in the context of mounting resource crunch confronting the state government, suggested a way to strengthen the finances of colleges in the private sector is by restructuring tuition fees so as to make those, who can afford, pay a reasonable price for the service while safeguarding the interest of the weaker sections through a liberal scheme of scholarship. Another suggestion, he made, is to abandon the 'Direct Payment Agreement' in stages and degree and thus to confer increasing autonomy on the private colleges.

Salim (1993) made a study of the private cost of higher education in Kerala. He divided the total private cost into academic and incidental. Academic cost components are pre-admission costs, fees paid to the college, private tuition fee, expenditure on books, stationery, project/thesis works, study tours and other instructional costs. Incidental cost, on the other hand consists of subscriptions, travel costs, hostel expenses, clothing, entertainment, donations and others. Salim found that actual cost per student in technical education was only slightly higher at the degree level and substantially lower at the post-graduate level than that of general education. It was also observed that the facilities of higher education were being appropriated mostly by high income and occupation group.

In another study, Salim (1996) attempted to estimate institutional costs of higher education in Kerala. The findings of this study can be summerised as (a) creation and maintenance of a seat in engineering education was much more expensive on the part of the institution/ government than doing the same in general education, (b) among the components of recurring cost, teaching cost was identified as the most important one, (c) building cost figures the most among the elements of capital cost, and (d) while a major part of institutional costs was liberally subsidized by the government, only a small portion is reaped from students' fee.

Baldev *et al.* (1994), based on a sample of 27 schools of urban and rural areas in Lunglei district, conducted a survey on school education in Mizoram. The study found that per pupil expenditure was the highest in the government middle school followed by primary schools. Expenditure in government aided middle school was found to be equal to that of government high school. However, the unit costs of education in government aided high schools are found to be marginally higher than in government high schools.

Vanlalchhawna (2006) conducted a study of higher educational cost in North-East India. The study was based on the functioning of the then NEHU affiliated colleges in Mizoram. The study examines the growth of public expenditure on higher education, sources of educational finances, unit institutional cost as well as private costs. Chhawna showed, among other things, that: (i) unit cost of education at the institutional level is dominated by unit recurring cost, (ii) there exists an inverse relationship between unit institutional cost and enrolment size, (iii) private cost is dominated by non-academic costs and is positively related with socio-economic status of the parents, (iv) institutional costs constitute less than one-third of the total costs, and (v) education is relatively expensive in government colleges as compared to private institutions. The study also found that unit cost per year increased for all levels of education between 1976 and 1991, and it increases as one moves from lower to higher stages of education. An interesting fact he observed is that, private cost, contrary to the general belief, is greater than institutional costs in Mizoram, and out of this institutional costs only 12 to 20 per cent was devoted to non-recurring items which may be regarded as capital formation. So, he came up with the suggestion that the state government should allocate more resources, perhaps not less than 20 per cent of its total budgetary expenditure to education.

REFERENCES

Agarwal, P.D. (1988). "Unit Cost in Conventional and Distance Education System," in B.K. Koul, *et al.*, (eds) *Studies in Distance Education*, AIU/IGNOU, New Delhi.

Baldev, Mahajan *et al.*, (1994). *Educational Administration in Mizoram: Structures, Processes and Future Prospects*, NIEPA, New Delhi.

Becker, Gary S. (1975). *Human Capital: A Theoretical and Empirical Analysis with Special Reference to Education*, 2nd Education, NBER, New York.

Bottomly, J.A. (1972). *Studies in Institutional Management in Higher Education – University of Bradford; Cost and Potential Economics.* O.E.C.D. Paris.

Blaug, M. and Woodhall, M. (1967). "Productivity Trends in British Secondary Education, 1950-63, in J. Hallak (ed) *Educational Costs and Productivity*, UNESCO, IIEP, Paris, (Mimeographed).

Blaug, M. *et al.*, (1969). *Causes of Graduate Unemployment in India.* The Penguin Press, London.

Chalam, K.S. (1986). *Finances Costs and Productivity of Higher Education.* Inter-India Publications, New Delhi.

Coombs and Hallak, (1972). *Managing Educational Costs,* UNESCO: IIEP Oxford University Press, New York.

Datt, Rudder (1969). "Unit Costs of Education – A Case Study of Haryana Colleges" in H.N. Pandit (ed) *Measurement of Cost Productivity and Efficiency of Education,* NCERT, New Delhi.

Datt, Rudder (1988). "Distance Education Versus Traditional Higher Education A Cost Comparison," in B.N. Koul (eds) *Studies in Distance Education,* AIU/IGNOU, New Delhi.

Dey, B. (1969). "On Costing of Education," in H.N. Pandit (ed) *Measurement of Cost Productivity and Efficiency of Education,* NCERT, New Delhi.

Government of India (1970). *Education and National Development* (Report of the Education Commission, 1964-66) NCERT, New Delhi.

Garg, V.P. (1982). Cost Analysis of the University of Punjab, 1950-51 to 1974-75. *Indian Educational Review,* July.

Graham, J.W. (1987). "International Educational Expenditures" in George Psacharopoulos (ed) *Economics of Education Research and Studies.* Pergamon Press, Oxford.

Hallak, J. (1969). *The Analysis of Educational Costs and Expenditure.* UNESCO: IIEP, Paris.

International Institute for Educational Planning (IIEP) (1972). *Educational Cost Analysis in Action: Case Studies for Planner, Vol – II & III.* UNESCO: IIEP, Paris.

Institute of Applied Manpower Research (IAMR) (1964). *Cost study 1964.* New Delhi.

Institute of Applied Manpower Research (1975). *Pattern of Expenditure and Per Student Cost in Indian Institute of Technology,* New Delhi.

Kulkarni, G.B. (1969). "Cost of Education in Commerce Colleges of Bombay 1962-63 to 1966-67" in H.N. Pandit (ed) *Measurement of Cost Productivity and Efficiency of Education,* NCERT, New Delhi.

Lalliani. (1990). *An Analystical study of the Primary Education in Mizoram during the Post-Independence period*; unpublished Ph.D. Thesis; Department of Education, NEHU, Shillong.

Machlup, F. (1962). *The Production and Distribution of Knowledge in United States,* Princeton University Press, New Jersey.

Mathew, E.T. (1991). *Financing Higher Education,* Concept Publishing Company, New Delhi.

Maynard, J. (1971). *Some Micro-economics of Higher Education: Economies of Scale,* University of Nebraska, Lincoln, Nebraska.

Mingat, Alain and Tan, J.P. (1985). "On Equity in Education again: An International Comparison" *Journal of Human Resources,* 20 Vol., No. 2 Spring.

Organisation for Economic Co-operation and Development (OECD) (1977). *Educational Expenditure in France, Japan and the United Kingdom,* OECD, Paris.

Panchamukhi, P.R. (1965). "Educational Capital in India", *Indian Economic Journal,* 12, January-March.

Pandit, H.N. (1972). "Cost and Financing of Education—Private and Social Participation", *Indian Educational Review,* July, Vol. 2, No. 2.

Prakash, S. (1977). *Educational System of India, An Econometric Study,* Concept Publishing Company, New Delhi.

Prakash, Shri and Chowdhury, Sumitra. (1994). *Expenditure on Education – Theory, Models and Growth,* NIEPA, New Delhi.

Psacharopoulos, G. (1972). *The Return to Education: An International Comparison,* Elseviern, Amsterdam.

Salim, A. Abdul (1993). "Private Cost of Higher Education in Kerala; Socio-Economic Analysis", *Journal of Higher Education,* Volume 16, No. 3, Summer.

Salim, A. Abdul (1996). "Institutional Cost of Higher Education – A Case Study of Kerala", *Manpower Journal,* Vol. XXXII. No. I, April-June.

Shah, K.R. (1969). "Private Costs of Elementary Education" in H.N. Pandit (ed) *Measurement of Cost Productivity and Efficiency of Education,* NCERT, New Delhi.

Shah, K.R. (1969). "Expenditure on Professional School Education in India, 1950-51 to 1960-61" in H.N. Pandit (ed) *Measurement of Cost Productivity and Efficiency of Education,* NCERT, New Delhi.

Sharma, G.D. (1980). *Institutional Costs of University Education – A Study of Costs and Efficiency of Indian University System,* AIU, New Delhi.

Sharma, G.D. and Mridula (1982). *Economics of College Education – A Study of Hindu College,* Delhi, AIU, New Delhi.

Sharma, Narayan Prasad (1993). *Economics of College Education. A Study of Non-Viable Colleges.* Anmol Publications, New Delhi.

Shultz, T.W. (1960). "Capital Formation by Education", *Journal of Political Economy,* Vol. 68, December.

Shultz, T.W. (1961). "Education and Economic Growth" in H.G. Richey (ed) *Social Forces influencing American Education,* Chicago.

Shultz, T.W. (1963). *The Economic Value of Education.* Columbia University Press, New York.

Tilak, J.B.G. (1987). *The Economics of Inequality in Education,* Sage Publication India Pvt. Ltd., New Delhi.

Tilak, J.B.G. (1993). "Unit Cost Analysis of Higher Education in India" in Devendra Thakur (ed)., *Education and Manpower Planning*, Deep & Deep Publication Pvt. Ltd., New Delhi.

Tilak, J.B.G. (1993). "Financing Higher Education in India" in Sumas Chitnis & Phillip G. Altbach, (eds) *Higher Education Reform in India* (*Experience and Perspective*), Sage Publication Pvt. Ltd., New Delhi.

Tilak, J.B.G. (1994). *Education for Development in Asia,* Sage Publication Pvt. Ltd., New Delhi.

Vaizey, J. (1958). *Costs of Education,* Allen & Unwin, London.

Vaizey, J. and Sheehan, J. (1968). *Resources for Education. An Economic Study of Education in the United Kingdom, 1920-1965*, Allen & Unwin, London.

Vanlalchhawna, (2006). *Higher Education in North-East India,* Mittal Publications, New Delhi.

4

Trend of Expenditure on Education in Mizoram

Introduction

Expenditure on education is globally considered as investment expenditure today. It brings returns both to the individual and to the society. This is reflected in the unprecedented growth of educational sector in terms of enrolment, variety of courses, educational institutions and the amounts of expenditure incurred by public authorities and private households. Thus, the study of the growth of educational expenditure has become an important part of the economics of education. This is more significant in the state of Mizoram where the government supports the system of education almost to the point of totality.

The extent of expenditure on education depends on the factors like literacy, enrolment, educational facilities etc. Accordingly, an attempt has been made in this chapter to examine the development of education in Mizoram. The first part of the chapter deals with the educational profile of the state which throws light on the variables that determine educational expenditure and the later part analyses the growth trend of public expenditure on education, in general and higher education, in particular.

Educational Profile of Mizoram

From the time when there was no formal education and no school in

Mizoram, young boys had to go through quite rigorous training and discipline at home and in the village community through the institution of the 'Zawlbuk' (bachelors' quarter) which was their learning centre. Very strict discipline was maintained in the 'Zawlbuk' for the inculcation of the moral ethics based on 'tlawmngaihna' (hospitability, kindness, unselfishness and helpfulness). The kind and range of activities carried out under the aegis of the 'Zawlbuk' served to a great extent as an informal education for the young men.

However, the formal education was founded in Mizoram only with the arrival of the two Christian missionaries, Rev. James Herbert Lorrain (Pu Buanga) and Dr. Frederick W. Savidge (Sap Upa) on 11th January, 1894 under Arthington Aborigines Mission. Their first important contribution for the people of Mizoram was preparation of Alphabets based on Roman scripts. The first primary school was started at Aizawl in 1898 and in rural areas in 1901. The early schools established by the missionaries were temporary and experimental in their functioning with no clear policy guidelines from authority (Hluna, J.V., 1992). The important landmarks in the field of education in Mizoram are given in Table 4.1. However, in 1993 the government

Table 4.1: Landmarks of Education in Mizoram

Sl. No.	*Events*	*Year*
1.	First Primary School at Aizawl	1898
2.	At Rural Areas	1901
3.	Opening of the First Upper Primary School	1907
4.	Opening of the First High School	1944
5.	Establishments of the First College	1958
6.	First PSLC Examination	1903
7.	First MSLC Examination	1909
8.	First Matriculation Examination	1948
9..	Establishments of the First College of Teachers Education	1975
10.	Establishment of Mizoram Board of School Education	1975
11.	Establishment of SCERT	1980
12.	Establishment of Mizoram University	2001
13.	Establishment of ICFAI in the State	2005
14.	Establishment six mini DIETs in the State	2005

Source: Singh (2008), Strategic Developmental Plan for Adoption of Information & Communication Technology (ICT) in College Libraries of Mizoram.

started giving grants-in-aid to schools maintained by the missionaries and also provide other incentives to the students, which marked the beginning of a new era in the expansion of education in villages on a regular basis. Within the first forty years of British administration the Mizos made a steady progress in the field of education in spite of the fact that the cost incurred by the government had never exceeded sixteen paise per head per year (McCall, 1977).

Although Mizoram is a late starter it has achieved remarkable progress in the field of education, occupying the status of the second literate state in India today. Through public expenditure and community participation this spectacular quantitative and qualitative expansion of education has come about in Mizoram.

Literacy

One of the important yardsticks to measure the educational attainment of a country or state is the level of its literacy. As per the report of the National Sample Survey Organization (NSSO), Mizoram was declared as the top most literate state among other states in India, with a literacy rate of 95 per cent. However, the latest survey (State of the States, '*India Today*', 2007) reveals that the literacy rate has been showing a decreasing trend over the years in the state. According to the 2001 Census Kerala topped in the literacy level among other states in India with 90.90 per cent literacy rate leaving Mizoram behind at the second position with 88.80 per cent literates.

The comparative rates of literacy for the State of Mizoram and the country as a whole are given in Table 4.2. In Mizoram the literacy rate is relatively high as compared to the all-India average. According to 2001 Census, the literacy rate of the state was 88.80 per cent, with male and female literacy rate being 90.71 and 86.75 per cent, respectively. However, the literacy rate for the country as a whole was only 65.38 per cent, with 75.85 per cent for male and 54.16 per cent for female as per the Census of 2001.

It is seen that the literacy rate in Mizoram had increased from 36.23 per cent in 1951 to 88.80 per cent in 2001, while at the national level the literacy rate rose from 18.33 per cent to 65.38 per cent during the same period. Table 4.2 also reveals that, female literacy rate in Mizoram was higher than the national average as well as the all-

Table 4.2: Literacy Rates in Mizoram and India, 1951 to 2001

(Percentage)

Year	Mizoram			India		
	Male	Female	Persons	Male	Female	Persons
1951	46.15	16.70	36.23	27.16	8.86	18.33
1961	53.40	34.70	44.00	40.40	15.35	28.30
1971	60.49	46.71	53.79	45.96	21.97	34.45
1981	79.36	68.61	74.26	56.38	29.76	43.57
1991	85.61	78.60	82.27	64.13	39.29	52.21
2001	90.71	86.75	88.80	75.85	54.16	65.38

Note: (1) Literacy rates for 1951, 1961 and 1971 Censuses relates to population aged five years and above. The rates for the 1981,1991 and 2001 Census relate to population aged seven years and above.

(2) The 1981 Literacy rates exclude Assam where census could not be conducted and the 1991 literacy rates exclude Jammu & Kashmir where Census could not be conducted due to disturbed conditions.

(3) The 2001 Census, literacy rates exclude entire Kachchh district, Morvi, Maliya-Miyana and Wankaner talukas of Rajkot district, Jodiya taluka of Jamnagar district of Gujarat State and entire Kinnaur district of Himachal Pradesh where population enumeration of Census of India, 2001, could not be conducted due to natural calamities.

Source : 1. Census of India 2001.

2. Economic Survey, Mizoram, 2008-09.

India female literacy rate as per 1961 Census. In the subsequent censuses of 1971, 1981, 1991 and 2001 the female literacy rate of Mizoram exceeded the national average as well as male and female literacy rates.

The district-wise literacy rate of Mizoram, as per 2001 Census, is presented in Table 4.3. The table shows that Aizawl district tops the rate of literacy at 96.50 per cent, while Lawngtlai district records the least at 64.70 per cent. Out of the eight districts of Mizoram four districts are seen to have literacy rate lower than the state-average of 88.80 per cent and another four districts above it. Below average districts are Lawngtlai (64.70%), Mamit (79.14%), Saiha (82.20%) and Lunglei (84.20%), while Champhai (91.20%), Kolasib (91.33%), Serchhip (95.10%) and Aizawl (96.50%) districts have literacy rates above the state-average rate.

Table 4.3: District-wise Literacy Rate in Mizoram (2001)

(Percentage)

Sl. No.	District	Male	Female	Persons
1.	Aizawl	96.75	96.26	96.50
2.	Serchhip	96.18	94.10	95.10
3.	Kolasib	92.34	90.22	91.33
4.	Champhai	92.15	89.10	91.20
5.	Lunglei	87.43	80.60	84.20
6.	Saiha	86.11	78.10	82.20
7.	Mamit	82.97	74.81	79.14
8.	Lawngtlai	70.90	57.81	64.70

Note: Literacy rates of 1951, 1961 and 1971 are crude literacy rates.
Source: *Statistical Abstract of Mizoram*, 2009.

Educational Infrastructure

In this section, the basic indicators of educational development, viz. the number of institutions, teachers and enrolment trends has been examined.

The enrolment trend as depicted in Table 4.4 shows that, the total number of students enrolled in various levels of education increased from 205321 in 2000-01 to 285499 in 2008-09, registering a growth rate of 3.37 per cent per annum. As for the percentage share of enrolment, primary level accounts for 50.30 to 53.20 per cent of the total during the same period. This enrolment in primary schools represents the highest share, while enrolment in professional colleges accounts for the least percentage to the total. Out of the total enrolment professional colleges constituted only 0.26 per cent in 2000-01, which has just halved to 0.13 per cent in 2008-09.

Between the period 2001-02 and 2008-09 enrolment in post-graduate level grew at an annual compound rate of 15.88 per cent, which is the highest rate among all levels of education in the state. In absolute terms, the number of students rose from 306 to 998 during the said period. The second highest growth rate is observed in case of enrolment in general degree colleges of under-graduate level. Number of students increased from 5201 to 7553 during the period 2000-01 to 2008-09, recording a growth rate of 5.38 per cent per annum. During the same period, from 651 students in professional colleges the

Table 4.4: Enrolment Trends in Mizoram (2000-01 to 2008-09)

Year	*Primary School*	*Middle School*	*High School*	*Hr. Sec. School*	*General Degree Colleges (Arts, Sc. & Com.)*	*Professional Colleges (MLC, CTE & MHTC)*	*Technical Institutions (MPL & WPA)*	*University (MZU)*	*Total*
1	2	3	4	5	6	7	8	9	10
2000-01	103269	48793	37197	9671	5201	539	651	N.A.	205321
2001-02	116226	53130	43030	9076	4867	446	337	306	227418
2002-03	116303	56490	39875	12555	5014	403	381	401	231422
2003-04	120217	58623	45200	16890	5826	344	436	435	247971
2004-05	102807	56038	43161	10283	5961	537	500	492	219779
2005-06	132046	88044	41610	10555	7462	505	503	543	281268
2006-07	130342	58533	44322	11762	6486	490	480	591	253006
2007-08	134656	57399	43675	12816	6548	411	513	743	256761
2008-09	151899	64887	44576	14649	7553	369	568	998	285499
CAGR (%)	3.92	3.13	1.51	3.55	5.38	–1.63	2.22	15.88	3.37

Note: General Degree Colleges include Pachhunga University College.

Sources: 1. *Statistical Abstract of Mizoram*, 2009.

2. Economic Survey, Mizoram, 2008-09.

enrolment has come down to 369 only, implying an annual growth rate of (-)1.63 per cent.

The growth of enrolment in absolute terms at the school level of education (columns 2-5) has been considerable as compared to that of the higher level of education (columns 6-9). This may be attributed among others to demographic pressure in the state. Very poor enrolment in professional education both in absolute and relative terms may be due to the concentration of all the three colleges in Aizawl, the state capital of Mizoram, which restricts the easy accessibility of students from far-flung areas.

Table 4.5 shows the rates of increase in educational institutions and teachers at each level of education. At primary level, the number of teachers increased from 4505 in 2000-01 to 8716 in 2008-09, registering an annual growth rate of 7.49 per cent, which is higher than the growth rate of schools at 4.49 per cent as the institutions rose from 1209 to 1783 during the same period. However, in case of middle, high and higher secondary schools, the number of teachers grew at a lower rate than that of the institutions. The number of schools grew by 6.47 per cent, 6.43 per cent and 14.41 per cent per annum at middle, high and higher secondary level, respectively. However, the teachers therein increased respectively by 5.40 per cent, 5.04 per cent and 10.37 per cent annually.

As for higher education, except in case of university, the number of teachers showed a declining trend over the period under consideration. However, the number of institutions declined in case of general and professional education, while it remained constant at 2 in case of polytechnics and 1 in case of university. Number of colleges for general education came down from 27 to 22 and for professional education from 4 to 3 between 2000-01 and 2008-09, registering a growth rate of (-)3.22 per cent and (-)4.68 per cent per year, respectively. This is due to withering away of some non-viable private colleges and amalgamation of some other colleges in 2004. University teachers grew at a rate of 29.12 per cent per annum, as the absolute number increased from only 24 in 2001-02 to 132 in 2008-09, which is the highest rate among all categories of teachers. At the other extreme, the annual growth rate of teachers is observed to be the lowest at (-)2.76 per cent in case of professional colleges as the number declined from 37 to 31 during the period under consideration.

Table 4.5: Number of Educational Institutions and Teachers in Mizoram (2000-01 to 2008-09)

Particulars	*2000-01*	*2001-02*	*2002-03*	*2003-04*	*2004-05*	*2005-06*	*2006-07*	*2007-08*	*2008-09*	*CAGR (%)*
Primary School										
Schools	1209	1377	1504	1504	1481	1688	1700	1752	1783	4.49
Teachers	4505	5429	5855	5861	5469	5210	8099	8002	8716	7.49
Middle School										
Schools	676	851	911	908	939	1121	1081	1090	1253	6.47
Teachers	4999	5747	5599	5608	7067	7983	7271	6846	7754	5.40
High School										
Schools	283	370	409	443	448	484	502	508	502	6.43
Teachers	2805	2853	2923	3108	3592	3694	3768	3935	3886	5.04
Hr. Sec. School										
Schools	30	33	47	71	67	76	80	82	86	14.41
Teachers	504	485	648	669	845	854	929	941	1058	10.37
Degree College										
Colleges	27	27	27	27	24	24	22	22	22	–3.22
Teachers	750	744	744	754	733	731	723	735	722	–0.46
Professional College										
Colleges	4	4	4	4	3	3	3	3	3	–4.68
Teachers	37	37	37	37	36	34	31	31	31	–2.76
Tech. Institution										
Polytechnics	2	2	2	2	2	2	2	2	2	0
Teachers	27	27	27	27	25	25	28	25	25	–0.90
University										
University	N.A.	1	1	1	1	1	1	1	1	0
Teachers	N.A.	24	31	56	65	80	128	122	132	29.12

Note: Degree Colleges include Pachhunga University College.

Source: Same as Table 4.1.

Inter-district Comparison of Educational Facilities

Educational facilities differ widely among the eight districts of Mizoram. Table 4.6 shows the district-wise comparison of the number of institutions, student enrolment and the number of teachers at all levels of education for the year 2008-09.

In terms of educational institutions, enrolment and teachers, at primary level, Aizawl district ranks first with 553 schools (31.02%), 54484 pupils (35.87%) and 2880 teachers (33.044%). This is followed by Lunglei and Lawngtlai districts. Serchhip district, has the least number of primary schools and teachers, i.e. 97 primary schools (5.44%) and 451 teachers (5.17%). Student enrolment in Mamit district is seen to be the lowest at 7041 (4.64%). However, the teacher-student ratio at 1:18 in Kolasib, Champhai, Serchhip, Lawngtlai and Saiha districts is not much below the ratio in Aizawl at 1:19. In Mamit and Lunglei districts there are 14 students against 1 teacher in primary schools.

At all other levels of school education (from middle to higher secondary stage) more or less same pattern is observed in the inter-district analysis of educational facilities. Based on the number of institutions, students and teachers, an overall ranking of the eight districts may be made as under: (i) Aizawl, Lunglei and Champhai occupies the first, second and third position, respectively at all levels of school education; (ii) at the middle school level, Lawngtlai, Kolasib, Saiha, Serchhip and Mamit may be placed at the fourth, fifth, sixth, seventh and eighth rank, respectively; (iii) at the high school stage, fourth, fifth, sixth, seventh and eighth position goes, respectively to Lawngtlai, Serchhip, Kolasib, Saiha and Mamit district; and (iv) at higher secondary level, Serchhip, Saiha, Kolasib, Mamit and Lawngtlai district may be ranked fourth, fifth, sixth, seventh and eighth, respectively.

At the undergraduate level of general education, with 10 out of 22 colleges, 5820 out of 7558 students and 418 out of 722 teachers in the state, Aizawl district represents the highest intensity of educational facilities. In terms of number of colleges and enrolment strength Lunglei occupies the second position, while it stands third in so far as the number of teachers is concerned. Kolasib remained in fourth position in the count of colleges and enrolment, and in sixth

Table 4.6: Inter District Comparison of Educational Facilities

Particulars	*Mamit*	*Kolasib*	*Aizawl*	*Champhai*	*Serchhip*	*Lunglei*	*Lawngtlai*	*Saiha*
Primary School								
Institution	98	124	553	180	97	353	247	131
Pupil	7041	11975	54484	15827	7974	21616	18554	14428
Teacher	478	671	2880	890	451	1527	1006	813
T-P Ratio	1:14	1:18	1:19	1:18	1:18	1:14	1:18	1:18
Middle School								
Institution	46	95	450	145	77	220	132	88
Pupil	2376	4933	26610	7101	4358	9399	6062	4048
Teacher	291	462	3213	787	437	1232	787	545
T-P Ratio	1:08	1:11	1:08	1:09	1:10	1:08	1:08	1:07
High School								
Institution	30	28	185	67	33	89	40	30
Pupil	1872	2922	19605	5221	3145	5965	3239	2607
Teacher	199	206	1569	491	239	685	287	210
T-P Ratio	1:09	1:14	1:12	1:11	1:13	1:09	1:11	1:12
Hr. Sec. School								
Institution	4	3	45	7	6	14	3	4
Pupil	202	593	9318	836	535	2095	363	707
Teacher	34	51	551	82	86	172	32	50
T-P Ratio	1:06	1:12	1:17	1:10	1:06	1:12	1:11	1:14
Degree College								
Institution	2	1	10	2	1	3	2	1
Pupil	76	207	5820	224	154	747	193	137
Teacher	38	35	418	55	22	63	67	24
T-P Ratio	1:02	1:06	1:14	1:04	1:07	1:12	1:03	1:06
Professional College								
Institution			3					
Pupil			369					
Teacher			31					
T-P Ratio			1:12					
Tech. Institution								
Institution			1			1		
Pupil			253			315		
Teacher			8			17		
T-P Ratio			1:32			1:19		
University								
Institution			1					
Pupil			998					
Teacher			132					
T-P Ratio			1:08					

Source: Compiled and computed from *Statistical Abstract of Mizoram*, 2009.

place regarding teacher strength. According to the number of colleges, Mamit, Champhai and Lawngtlai may simultaneously be placed in third rank, while Saiha and Serchhip remains at the fourth place. Champhai with 224 students remained in the third rank, Lawngtlai with 193 students in fifth, Serchhip with 154 students in sixth, Saiha with 137 students in seventh and Mamit with 76 students stands at the eighth place. Looking at the number of teachers, Lawngtlai, Champhai, Mamit, Saiha and Serchhip may be placed at the second, fourth, fifth, seventh and eighth place, respectively. However, in terms of teacher-student ratio the districts come in the following order – Aizawl (1:14), Lunglei (1:12), Serchhip (1:07), Kolasib and Saiha (1:06), Champhai (1:04), Lawngtlai (1:03) and Mamit (1:02).

Educational facilities in the technical front are better in Lunglei than in Aizawl. Although there is one polytechnic in each of the two districts, Lunglei has 315 students (55.46%) and 17 teachers (68%) as against 253 students (44.54%) and 8 teachers (32%) in Aizawl. However, there are 32 and 19 students per teacher in Aizawl and Lunglei district, respectively.

As for the professional education, Aizawl has all the 3 colleges with 369 pupils and 31 teachers. The teacher-student ratio is, thus, 1:12. Similarly, with the lone university at Aizawl is the sole provider of post-graduate education in Mizoram. It has a teacher-student ratio of 1:08 as there are 132 teachers for 998 students.

Thus, except for technical institutions, Aizawl district is seen to comprise the highest number of educational facilities in all respects and at all levels. Further, as the stages of education increase less and less decentralization of educational infrastructure in the state is observed. The corollary is that the number of institutions, pupils and teachers are getting concentrated in Aizawl district as the level of education increases.

Professional and Vocational Education

In Mizoram professional and vocational education encompasses the areas like paramedical, agro-forestry, law, teachers training, engineering and technology, management and computer education. However, this diversification is a recent one and the facilities and levels are mostly inadequate.

In the field of medicine, Mizoram has no Medical College. But there are some paramedical institutions in the state. The Regional Institute of Paramedical and Nursing Sciences (RIPANS), Aizawl, funded by the North Eastern Council (NEC), offers degree and diploma courses in Nursing, Pharmacy and Medical Laboratory Technology. At present there are 346 students enrolled in these programmes. Mizoram College of Nursing, funded by the State Government offers B.Sc. Nursing course and has currently 89 students on its rolls. These apart, there are four other nursing schools in the state. These are: (i) Nursing School, Presbyterian Hospital, Durtlang, Aizawl; (ii) Nursing School, Civil Hospital, Lunglei; (iii) Apollo School of Nursing, Aizawl; and (iv) School of Nursing, Christian Hospital, Serkawn, Lunglei.

As to the field of agriculture, there is no Agriculture College in the State but the Central Agricultural University (CAU) with its headquarters at Imphal covers all the States in the North-East by having a campus in each State. The College of Veterinary Sciences of CAU is located at Aizawl and offers undergraduate, post-graduate and research courses. The State Government, under Animal Husbandry and Veterinary Department, has a School of Animal Husbandry and Veterinary Sciences which provide training to Veterinary Field Assistant (VFA). The Department of Agriculture has an Integrated Training Centre (ITC) at Hnahthial which provides basic agricultural training of two years duration mostly to the in-service personnel. The Krishi Vigyan Kendra (KVK) under the same Department gives training to farmers. Indian Council of Agricultural Research (ICAR) has one sub-centre in Mizoram. Regarding education in forestry, the Mizoram University has established the Department of Forestry and the Department of Horticulture, Aromatic and Medicinal Plants (HAMP) to offer post-graduate and research programmes. In addition to these the Government of Mizoram, under Forest and Environment Department, runs the Forest Education and Research Institute to impart training to foresters and forest guards.

As discussed earlier, Mizoram has at present only one Law College, viz. Mizoram Law College, Aizawl. There is no institution for post-graduation level of study in law in the state.

Other than the College of Teachers Education (CTE) and Mizoram Hindi Training College (MHTC), discussed above, there are two District Institutes of Education and Training (DIETs), one each in Aizawl and Lunglei district. Of late, six other Mini DIETs are there in six district headquarters.

At present only Mizoram University (MZU) offers engineering and technology courses at the undergraduate level. For diploma levels of technical education there are two polytechnics, as mentioned earlier, in the state. For lower level technical training there are three Industrial Training Institutes (ITIs), one each in Aizawl, Lunglei and Saiha.

As for management education, the MZU and the Institute of Chartered Financial Analysts of India (ICFAI) University are offering MBA programme. The ICFAI University also offers Bachelor of Business Administration (BBA) and Bachelor of Hospitality and Tourism Management (BHTM) Courses.

In the field of computer education, Bachelor of Computer Application (BCA) course is offered by the ICFAI University, Department of Electronic Accreditation of Computer Courses (DoEACC), five State Government Colleges and one private institute, namely Higher and Technical Institution of Mizoram (HATIM), affiliated to MZU. Two other centres for IT education in the state are: Golden Republic Information Technology Centre (GRITC), Aizawl and Academic of Computer and Electronic Centre (AC & EC), Lunglei.

Open and Distance Learning

For the last two decades higher education through ODL has been there in the state of Mizoram. The first Study Centre (SC) of Indira Gandhi National Open University (IGNOU) in the state was set-up under Regional Centre (RC) of IGNOU at Shillong in 1989. However, with the establishment of RC, Aizawl in December 2000, the ODL system got further impetus. The RC is headed by a Regional Director who is assisted by one Assistant Regional Director, three Consultants and two Research and Technical Assistants.

The RC has a reference library with a collection of nearly 1000 volumes. The library has been selected for automation as a part of modlibnet. The RC is also equipped with facilities for instructional interaction through teleconferencing using Gyandarshan Edusat channels. The students attend these programmes as per schedule notified by the IGNOU. In addition, students also attend Video Counselling sessions at the RC on week days. The RC also has Tele-learning centre through which Computer Literacy and Computer Applications are offered.

All the eight districts in Mizoram have ODL facilities offered by IGNOU. At present, the Aizawl Regional Centre has 37 Study Centres out of which 13 are regular Study Centres attached to degree colleges and 14 are programme Study Centres for specialized programmes like teacher education, nursing, etc. The remaining are special Study Centres meant for specific sections of the society like minorities, Jail inmates, etc. There are as many as 354 Academic Counsellors on the panel of the RC for providing Counselling support to the students through contact classes which are conducted on Saturdays at the Study Centres. The average attendance of students is a little over 50 per cent.

The enrolment of students under RC, Aizawl has substantially increased during the past few years. It increased from 403 in 2001, to 5921 in 2009. The female students account for around 45 per cent in the total enrolment. The majority of students are in the age group 18-25 years. The Bachelor Preparatory Programme, the Bachelor degree programmes followed by Master degree programmes have proved to be the most popular programmes in the region. The RC is currently offering a total of 59 programmes consisting of 12 Master's degree, 9 Bachelor's degree, 9 Diploma Programmes, 2 Post-graduate Certificate Programmes and 18 Certificate Programmes. The Distance Education Council (DEC) of IGNOU has selected ten colleges and given them the option to enroll their students for Certificate/Diploma programmes of IGNOU as a part of value added programme. Two institutions have been selected for functioning as Community Colleges.

Growth of Educational Expenditure in Mizoram

The system of education is largely owned, operated and financed by the government and in the present case by the State Government of Mizoram. Grants from the Central Government and international agencies are very limited and hence are excluded from the study of the present chapter. It concentrates on the expenditure on education by the government of the state, which it spends through the State Budgets.

Growth of Public Expenditure on Education

The growth of total budgetary expenditure as well as the expenditure on school education and higher education for the period 1997-98 to 2009-10 is given in Table 4.7 at current prices and in Table 4.8 at constant prices.

Table 4.7: Trend of Educational Expenditure in Mizoram (at Current Prices), 1997-98 to 2009-10

(In ₹ Lakhs)

Year	Total Budgetary Expenditure	Expenditure on School Education	Expenditure on Hr.&Tech. Education	Total Educational Expenditure
1	2	3	4	5
1997-98	85116.38	8531.85	1030.00	9561.85
1998-99	88252.00	9454.95	1188.50	10643.45
1999-00	101456.60	10019.86	1161.88	11181.74
2000-01	108739.50	10960.25	1441.20	12401.45
2001-02	121761.30	14854.40	3163.87	18018.27
2002-03	157739.10	16410.64	3026.11	19436.75
2003-04	138097.70	15218.45	2533.20	17751.65
2004-05	154083.10	15977.80	3034.02	19011.82
2005-06	180210.70	19209.40	3231.52	22440.92
2006-07	203669.60	20549.70	3007.26	23556.96
2007-08	232292.30	23689.04	3415.10	27104.14
2008-09	262503.60	25991.85	4122.05	30113.90
2009-10	386740.60	37993.19	6596.36	44589.55
CAGR	11.92	11.51	14.05	11.81

Notes: 1. The figures in the table represent budget estimates as actual figures of total budgetary expenditure for certain years could not be ascertained due to the use of different formats in different years by the Department.

2. Total Educational Expenditure in column 5 (= 3 + 4) excludes expenditure on Adult Education, Sports and Youth Services and Art and Culture.

Source: *State Budgets*, 1997-98 to 2009-10.

From the analysis of the tables following points may be observed regarding the trend of expenditures:

(i) Public expenditure on education has been continually increasing, except the reversals in 2003-04 and 2004-05, during the period under consideration. In nominal terms it increased 4.7 times over the period, i.e., from ₹ 9561.85 lakhs in 1997-98 to ₹ 44589.55 lakhs in 2009-10. This shows an annual growth rate of 11.81 per cent. However, in real terms the expenditure on education rose only 2.5 times, increasing at the rate of 6.37 per cent per annum during the said period.

Table 4.8: Growth of Public Expenditure on Education

(In ₹ Lakhs)

Year	*Total Budgetary Expenditure*	*Expenditure on School Education*	*Expenditure on Hr. & Tech. Education*	*Total Educational Expenditure*
1	2	3	4	5
1997-98	64093.66	6424.59	775.60	7200.19
1998-99	62723.53	6719.94	844.71	7564.64
1999-00	69825.62	6895.98	799.64	7695.62
2000-01	69839.14	7039.34	925.63	7964.97
2001-02	75487.47	9209.18	1961.48	11170.66
2002-03	94567.80	9838.51	1814.21	11652.73
2003-04	78509.22	8651.76	1440.14	10091.90
2004-05	82265.38	8530.59	1619.87	10150.46
2005-06	92132.28	9820.76	1652.11	11472.86
2006-07	98772.86	9965.91	1458.42	11424.33
2007-08	107692.29	10982.40	1583.26	12565.67
2008-09	112229.00	11112.38	1762.31	12874.69
2009-10	159218.02	15641.49	2715.67	18357.16
CAGR	6.46	6.08	8.49	6.37

Source: Computed from Table 4.1 (deflating by the Wholesale Price Index).

(ii) While expenditure on school education increased from ₹ 8531.85 lakhs to ₹ 37993.19 lakhs registering a growth rate of 11.51 per cent per year, the amount incurred on higher education rose from ₹ 1030.00 lakhs to ₹ 6596.36 lakhs, showing an annual compound growth rate of 14.05 per cent during the period under consideration. At constant prices, the annual growth rates of public expenditure on school education and higher education were 6.08 and 8.49 per cent, respectively.

(iii) Total budgetary expenditure was ₹ 85116.38 lakhs in 1997-98 which has increased 4.5 fold, i.e. to ₹ 386740.60 lakhs in 2009-10. The amount grew nearly at the rate of 12 per cent per annum. But in real terms the growth rate was lower at 6.46 per cent per year, as the amount of budget expenditure rose from ₹ 64093.66 lakhs in 1997-98 to ₹ 159218.02 lakhs in 2009-10, implying a 2.5 times hike during the same period.

Growth of Expenditure on Higher Education

Public expenditure on higher education in Mizoram at current and constant prices during the period 1997-98 to 2009-10 is given in Table 4.9. A look into the table shows that the amount spent on higher education in each successive year has not increased continuously. However, the expenditure at current prices rose from ₹ 1030.00 lakhs

Table 4.9: Growth of Expenditure on Higher Education in Mizoram (1997-98 to 2009-10)

(In ₹ Lakhs)

Year	*At Current Prices*	*Index of Growth*	*At Constant Prices (1993-94=1000*	*Index of Growth*
1	*2*	*3*	*4*	*5*
1997-98	1030.00	100.00	775.60	100.00
1998-99	1188.50	115.40	844.71	108.88
1999-00	1161.88	112.82	799.64	103.07
2000-01	1441.20	139.94	925.63	119.31
2001-02	3163.87	307.21	1961.48	252.83
2002-03	3026.11	293.84	1814.21	233.85
2003-04	2533.20	245.97	1440.14	185.63
2004-05	3034.02	294.60	1619.87	208.80
2005-06	3231.52	313.78	1652.11	212.96
2006-07	3007.26	292.00	1458.42	187.99
2007-08	3415.10	331.61	1583.26	204.08
2008-09	4122.05	400.25	1762.31	227.16
2009-10	6596.36	640.51	2715.67	350.05

Source: Derived from Tables 4.1 and 4.2.

However, the expenditure at current prices rose from ₹ 1030.00 lakhs in 1997-98 to ₹ 6596.36 lakhs in 2009-10. The index of growth (in column 3) has risen from 100 to 640.51, meaning that the expenditure has increased 6.4 times over the period.

In real terms the expenditure during the same period increased from ₹ 775.60 lakhs to ₹ 2715.67 lakhs. This implies a mere 3.5 times hike in the amount spent, as the index of growth (in column 5) rose from 100 to 350.05 only.

From the foregoing analysis it may be observed that, during the period 2000-01 to 2008-09 the variations in enrolment (Table 4.4), number of institutions and teachers (Table 4.5) in the higher education sector were negligible. But the variation in public expenditure was considerable, especially between 2000-01 and 2004-05, and again between 2007-08 and 2009-10 (Table 4.9). This implies that the public authorities do not follow any guiding principle while spending on higher education.

Relevant Expenditure Ratios of Higher Education

The rise in public expenditure on higher education can be said to be a function of the following variables:

1. State's capacity to spend on higher education, and
2. State's willingness to increase the allocation on this sector.

The growth of higher education expenditure has been guided by and often designed to realize the plan objectives of achieving higher educational goals in the state. Temporal increases in higher educational expenditures may be conceived largely by the concept of growth. It is seldom an indication of qualitative development for which the study of other educational and academic parametres is necessary.

The state's capacity to spend on education, or for that matter any public service, is determined by State Domestic Product (SDP) or state's income, which is, of course, only a necessary but not sufficient condition to spend more on any particular sector. Total expenditure shows in a sense the 'effort' of the government for the development of any service like education (agriculture, industry or health).

Higher educational expenditure is, therefore, juxtaposed to total educational expenditure, total budgetary expenditure and Net State

Table 4.10: Ratio of Higher Educational Expenditure in Mizoram (1997-98 to 2009-10)

(Percentage)

Year	*Of Total Educational Expenditure*	*Of Total Budgetary Expenditure*	*Of NSDP (State Income)*
1	2	3	4
1997-98	10.77	1.21	NA
1998-99	11.17	1.35	NA
1999-00	10.39	1.15	0.82 (R)
2000-01	11.62	1.33	0.99 (R)
2001-02	17.56	2.60	2.03 (R)
2002-03	15.57	1.92	1.78 (R)
2003-04	14.27	1.83	1.44 (R)
2004-05	15.96	1.97	1.65
2005-06	14.40	1.79	1.74
2006-07	12.77	1.48	1.48
2007-08	12.60	1.47	1.57 (Q)
2008-09	13.69	1.57	1.78 (A)
2009-10	14.79	1.71	2.65 (P)

Note: NA = Not Available (R) = Revised (A) = Advance (Q) = Quick (P) = Provisional

Source: 1. Computed from data available in Table 4.1

2. *Statistical Abstract of Mizoram*, 2009, Directorate of Economics and Statistics.

Domestic Product (NSDP) to get the relevant expenditure ratios. This is shown in Table 4.10.

The table reveals that:

(a) The ratio of higher educational expenditure to total educational expenditure was at its lowest level of 10.39 per cent in 1999-2000 and it touched its highest level in 2001-02 with the figure reading at 17.56 per cent.

(b) When the ratio of higher educational expenditure to total educational expenditure touched 17.56 per cent level in 2001-02, its share in total state budgetary expenditure went up to 2.60 per cent which was as low as 1.15 per cent in 1999-2000.

(c) Except for the year 2001-02, for all the years under consideration, the ratio of higher educational expenditure to total budgetary expenditure remained between the range of 1.15 per cent and 1.92 per cent.

(d) Higher educational expenditure as a ratio of state's income (NSDP) was as low as 0.82 per cent in 1999-2000, which continually increased to 2.03 per cent in 2001-02. After that, it started declining and reached 1.48 per cent in 2006-07. Since then, the ratio continued to improve until it reached the highest figure at 2.65 per cent in 2009-10.

Plan and Non-Plan Expenditure on Higher Education

In the accounting of budgetary expenditure, an important classification is attempted to as between plan and non-plan expenditure. As the nomenclature shows plan expenditure is aimed to finance plan programmes of higher education (as in other cases) and non-plan expenditure is expected to meet non-plan needs or committed expenditure on higher education. Often plan expenditure is called development expenditure and non-plan is dubbed as non-developmental expenditure. But, as Carl Shoup has once pointed out that, in education, even non-developmental expenditure is of 'instrumental value'.

With the above reason in mind the analysis of plan and non-plan expenditure on higher education in Mizoram is attempted in Table 4.11, which presents the relevant data and their respective ratios to total higher educational expenditure from 1997-98 to 2009-10.

The said table brings out the following points:

(i) In the year 1997-98 the total plan expenditure on higher education was ₹ 340.00 lakhs, constituting only 31.01 per cent of the total and non-plan expenditure was of the order of ₹ 690.00 lakhs, i.e. 66.99 per cent of the total.

(ii) By the year 2009-10 the share of plan expenditure increased to 58.86 per cent of the total, i.e. ₹ 3862.51 lakhs and the share of non-plan expenditure went down to 41.44 per cent with the absolute amount being ₹ 2733.85 lakhs only.

(iii) During the period under consideration, the lowest share of plan expenditure was recorded at 31.15 per cent in 1999-2000 and that of the non-plan expenditure was 35.00 per cent in 2001-02. The corollary is that, with 68.85 per cent share non-plan expenditure was the highest in 1999-2000 and with the share of 65.00 per cent of the total higher educational expenditure in 2001-02 plan expenditure was seen to be the highest.

(iv) On the whole, in the 13-year period between 1997-98 and 2009-10, plan expenditure on higher education in Mizoram grew at a compound rate of 19.46 per cent, while non-plan expenditure went up by 10.03 per cent and total educational expenditure rose by 14.05 per cent per annum.

Table 4.11: Plan and Non-Plan Expenditure on Higher Education in Mizoram (1997-98 to 2009-10)

(In ₹ Lakhs)

Year	*Plan*	*Non-Plan*	*Total*
1997-98	340.00 (33.01)	690.00 (66.99)	1030.00 (100)
1998-99	409.50 (34.46)	779.00 (65.54)	1188.50 (100)
1999-00	361.88 (31.15)	800.00 (68.85)	1161.88 (100)
2000-01	567.20 (39.36)	874.00 (60.64)	1441.20 (100)
2001-02	2056.40 (65.00)	1107.47 (35.00)	3163.87 (100)
2002-03	1636.97 (54.09)	1389.14 (45.91)	3026.11 (100)
2003-04	1393.35 (55.00)	1139.85 (45..00)	2533.20 (100)
2004-05	1671.10 (55.08)	1362.92 (44.92)	3034.02 (100)
2005-06	1775.40 (54.94)	1456.12 (45.06)	3231.52 (100)
2006-07	1533.30 (50.99)	1473.96 (49.01)	3007.26 (100)
2007-08	1846.40 (54.07)	1568.70 (45.93)	3415.10 (100)
2008-09	2265.30 (54.96)	1856.75 (45.04)	4122.05 (100)
2009-10	3862.51 (58.56)	2733.85 (41.44)	6596.36 (100)
CAGR	19.46	10.03	14.05

Note: Figures in brackets represent percentage to the total.

Source: Same as Table 4.1.

Public Expenditure on University Education

In Mizoram, regular courses are offered at the post-graduate level only in Mizoram University. This is a Central University constituted under an Act of Parliament (Mizoram University Act, 2000) on 2nd July, 2001. It receives fund under plan and non-plan heads, which is shown in Table 4.12.

Table 4.12: Plan and Non-Plan Expenditure in Mizoram University (2001-02 to 2009-10)

(*In ₹ Lakhs*)

Year	*Plan*	*Non-Plan*	*Total*
2001-02	N.A.	N.A.	N.A.
2002-03	295.13 (29.92)	691.22 (70.08)	986.35 (100)
2003-04	853.03 (52.47)	772.87 (47.53)	1625.90 (100)
2004-05	1309.80 (60.66)	849.46 (39.34)	2159.26 (100)
2005-06	2102.00 (68.47)	967.86 (31.53)	3069.86 (100)
2006-07	2516.86 (66.50)	1267.72 (33.50)	3784.58 (100)
2007-08	1301.67 (37.74)	2147.46 (62.26)	3449.13 (100)
2008-09	4135.79 (57.33)	3078.11 (42.67)	7213.90 (100)
2009-10	3226.28 (43.99)	4108.35 (56.01)	7334.63 (100)
CAGR	34.40	30.62	31.67

Note: Figures in brackets represent percentage to the total.
Source: Finance Department, Mizoram University.

An analysis of the table shows that:

(a) Plan expenditure in Mizoram University has increased from ₹ 295.13 lakhs in 2002-03 to ₹ 3226.28 lakhs in 2009-10, registering a growth rate of 34.40 per cent per year.

(b) The shares of plan expenditure to the total, however, were 29.92 per cent and 43.99 per cent in 2002-03 and 2009-10, respectively.

(c) As for the non-plan expenditure it is seen to have gone up from ₹ 691.22 lakhs in 2002-03 to ₹ 4108.35 lakhs in 2009-10, showing a growth rate of 30.62 per cent per annum.

(d) The relative share of non-plan expenditure to the total expenditure was 70.08 per cent in 2002-03 and in 2009-10 it came down to 56.01 per cent.

(e) During the 8 years period (2002-03 to 2009-10) under study, total expenditure showed an annual compound growth rate of 31.67 per cent.

The table also reveals that, in 5 out of 8 years (i.e., in 2003-04 to 2006-07 and in 2008-09) plan expenditures were higher than the non-plan expenditures. This is due to the fact that Mizoram University is still in its formative stage and developmental expenditures are prominent.

REFERENCES

Government of India : Census of India, 1951-2001.

Government of Mizoram : *Economic Survey, Mizoram, 2008-09*, Planning and Programme Implementation Department.

Government of Mizoram : *Statistical Abstract of Mizoram, 2009*, Directorate of Economics and Statistics.

Hluna, J.V. (1992), *Education and Missioneries in Mizoram*, Spectrum Publication, Guwahati/Delhi.

India Today (2007) : "State of the States", Volume XXXII, No. 38, 18-24 September.

McCall, A.G. (1977), *Lushai Chrysalis*, Tribal Research Institute, Aizawl.

Singh, S. (2008), "Strategic Developmental Plan for Adoption of Information and Communication Technology (ICT) in College Libraries of Mizoram", (Unpublished Ph.D. Thesis), Department of Library and Information Sciences, Mizoram University, Aizawl.

5

Analysis of Costs of Higher Education in Mizoram

Introduction

Educational institutions transform inputs into outputs incurring costs like any other firm or industry. Costs of higher education in Mizoram, as elsewhere, assume various forms. They may be real and monetary, explicit and implicit, quantifiable or measurable and non-quantifiable or non-measurable. Further, from the viewpoint of ownership it may be said that there are public costs of higher education and private costs as well. Without going into the complexity of the various concepts of costs in higher education, this chapter concentrates on the public costs of higher education measured in terms of public money spent on higher education and private costs measured in terms of students' fees, expenditures on books, accommodation, food, conveyance and personal maintenance.

Analysis of costs of higher education in Mizoram with their composition would be helpful in understanding and analyzing the financial burden on private shoulders and on the government. It also helps to assess to the extent to which the capacity of people has been tapped in financing higher education, and whether there is any scope for raising fees. Unit cost analysis can be used for allocating resources to the various institutions of higher education. Cost analysis is also useful in making policy decisions regarding cost curtailment, better utilization of resources etc.

In this chapter, the analysis of public cost of education is based on the primary data collected from the general degree colleges, professional colleges and technical institutions for the period 1997-98 to 2007-08, and the analysis of private cost is done on the basis of the data collected in the year 2007-08 from the students pursuing different courses of study in these higher educational institutions, including Mizoram University and ICFAI University, Mizoram. Attempts are also made in this chapter to study the relationship between unit cost of education and enrolment size, and to find out the optimum enrolment size for different institutions of higher education in the state.

Public Cost of Higher Education in Mizoram

Per unit public cost of higher education in Mizoram at current and constant prices are estimated and presented in Table 5.1 and Table 5.2, respectively. Public expenditure at current prices rose by 13.84 per cent per annum, while the annual growth rate of unit cost per student was 14.64 per cent during the period 1997-98 to 2007-08. Public expenditure continually has been on an increase during the period under study. It increased 3.72 times from ₹ 1010.00 lakhs in 1997-98 to ₹ 3759.74 lakhs in 2007-08. However, per unit pubic cost also has been increasing continuously from ₹ 13760.22 in 1997-98 to ₹ 58810.26 in 2007-08, except for the three years, 2003-04, 2004-05 and 2005-06. This is due to an increase in enrolment during these academic years.

In terms of constant prices (1993-94=100), the compound annual growth rate of public expenditure was only 8.48 per cent and that of unit cost per student was 9.24 per cent. Public expenditure increased 2.29 times from ₹ 760.54 lakhs to ₹ 1743.04 lakhs and unit cost by 2.63 times from ₹ 10361.61 to ₹ 27264.84 during the period 1997-98 to 2007-08. Per unit public cost was the highest at ₹ 29041.64 for the year 2002-03. Public expenditure for the corresponding year, i.e. ₹ 1428.85, however, was not low as compared to the two succeeding and all preceding years. It is, rather, the least enrolment which is responsible for the highest unit cost for this particular year.

Figure 5.1 portrays the trend of per unit public cost at current prices in panel 'A' and at constant prices in panel 'B'. An upward

Table 5.1 : Unit Cost of Higher Education in Mizoram at Current Prices (1997-98 to 2007-08)

Year	General Degree Colleges			Professional Colleges			Technical Institutions			Mizoram		
	Expen-diture (in ₹ lakhs)	*Enrol-ment*	*Unit cost (in ₹)*	*Expen-diture (in ₹ lakhs)*	*Enrolment*	*Unit cost (in ₹)*	*Expen-diture (in ₹ lakhs)*	*Enrol-ment*	*Unit cost (in ₹)*	*Expen-diture (in ₹ lakhs)*	*Enrol-ment*	*Unit cost (in ₹)*
1997-98	847.74	6604	12836.766	76.02	609	12482.759	86.24	127	67905.51	1010.00	7340	13760.218
1998-99	1048.64	6373	16454.417	87.29	552	15813.406	111.00	173	64161.85	1246.93	7098	17567.343
1999-00	1193.57	5803	20568.154	73.02	366	19950.820	104.44	157	66522.29	1371.03	6326	21672.937
2000-01	1406.51	4909	28651.66	105.88	473	22384.778	124.00	165	75151.52	1636.39	5547	29500.451
2001-02	1916.26	4570	41931.291	127.14	457	27820.569	155.45	337	46127.60	2198.85	5364	40992.729
2002-03	2093.98	4162	50311.869	147.12	377	39023.873	142.22	381	37328.08	2383.32	4920	48441.463
2003-04	2129.66	4763	44712.576	133.16	329	40474.164	148.64	436	34091.74	2411.46	5528	43622.648
2004-05	2309.75	4821	47910.185	158.82	424	37457.547	164.84	500	32968.00	2633.41	5745	45838.294
2005-06	2645.85	5943	44520.444	172.62	506	34114.625	183.40	503	36461.23	3001.87	6952	43179.948
2006-07	3214.29	5352	60057.735	187.25	491	38136.456	243.20	480	50666.67	3644.74	6323	57642.575
2007-08	3243.69	5469	59310.477	198.40	411	48272.506	317.65	513	61920.08	3759.74	6393	58810.261
CAGR (%)	14.27	-1.41	15.91	10.81	-1.81	12.85	11.39	16.74	-4.58	13.84	-0.70	14.64

Source: Field Survey, 2009.

Table 5.2: Unit Cost of Higher Education in Mizoram at Constant Prices (1993-94 = 100)

Year	General Degree Colleges			Professional Colleges			Technical Institutions			Mizoram		
	Expenditure (in ₹ lakhs)	Enrol-ment	Unit cost (in ₹)	Expen-diture (in ₹ lakhs)	Enrol-ment	Unit cost (in ₹)	Expen-diture (in ₹ lakhs)	Enrol-ment	Unit cost (in ₹)	Expen-diture (in ₹ lakhs)	Enrol-ment	Unit cost (in ₹)
1997-98	638.3584337	6604	9666.239154	57.24	609	9399.667636	64.94	127	51133.67	760.54	7340	10361.60993
1998-99	745.3020611	6373	11694.68164	62.04	552	11239.09438	78.89	173	45601.88	886.23	7098	12485.67371
1999-00	821.4521679	5803	14155.64653	50.25	366	13730.77748	71.88	157	45782.72	943.59	6326	14915.99249
2000-01	903.3461785	4909	18401.837	68.00	473	14376.86449	79.64	165	48266.87	1050.99	5547	18946.98182
2001-02	1188.009919	4570	25995.84069	78.82	457	17247.71787	96.37	337	28597.39	1363.21	5364	25413.96733
2002-03	1255.383693	4162	30162.99118	88.20	377	23395.60712	85.26	381	22378.95	1428.85	4920	29041.64473
2003-04	1210.722001	4763	25419.31558	75.70	329	23009.75789	84.50	436	19381.32	1370.93	5528	24799.68638
2004-05	1233.182061	4821	25579.38313	84.79	424	19998.69043	88.01	500	17601.71	1405.99	5745	24473.19496
2005-06	1352.684049	5943	22760.9633	88.25	506	17441.01457	93.76	503	18640.71	1534.70	6952	22075.63815
2006-07	1558.821532	5352	29125.96286	90.81	491	18494.88662	117.94	480	24571.61	1767.58	6323	27954.69191
2007-08	1503.79694	5469	27496.7442	91.98	411	22379.46504	147.26	513	28706.57	1743.04	6393	27264.84062
CAGR (%)	8.90	-1.41	10.45	5.59	-1.81	7.54	6.15	16.74	-9.07	8.48	-0.70	9.24

Source: Field Survey, 2009.

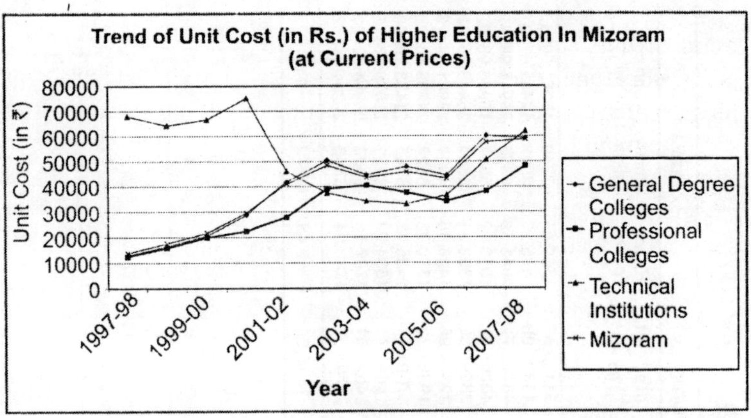

(A)

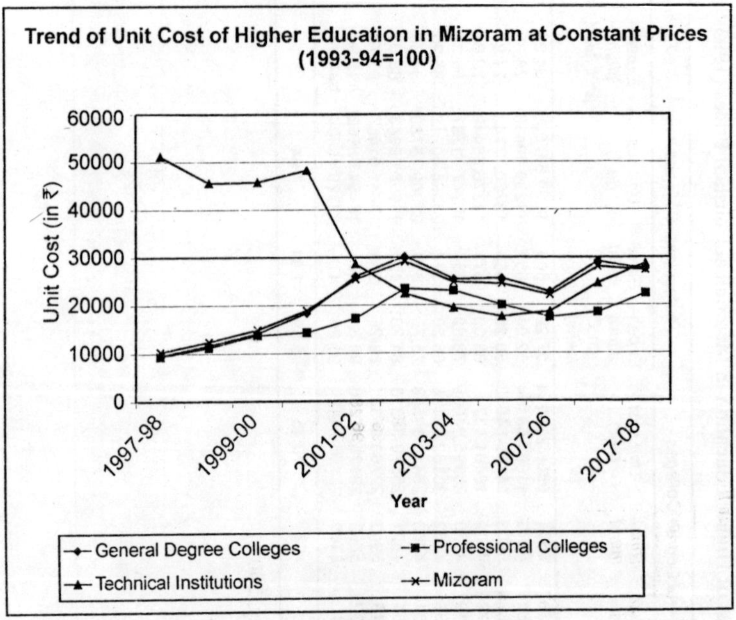

(B)

Fig. 5.1. (A) Trend of Unit Cost (in Rs.) of Higher Education In Mizoram (at Current Prices). (B) Trend of Unit Cost of Higher Education in Mizoram at Constant Prices (1993-94=100)

trend of unit cost is observed for the state as a whole, and for professional and general degree colleges, as well, with the slope being bit steeper in case of the ones at current prices than at constant prices.

The trend line of unit cost per student for technical institutions showed a wide variation, both at current and constant prices. It was exorbitantly high till the year 2000-01 starting from 1997-98, then sharply declined up to 2004-05, and marginally increased by 2007-08.

Growth Trend of per Unit Public Cost

Estimates of per unit public cost of higher education in Mizoram is given in Table 5.3. The compound annual growth rate is recorded at 14.64 per cent at current prices, while it was 9.24 per cent at constant prices. The annual growth rates as given by percentage increment over the previous year had fluctuated widely from year to year, registering even negative growth rates for two years at current prices and for four years at constant prices. The index of growth of per

Table 5.3: Growth Trend of Per Unit Public Cost in Mizoram (1997-98 to 2007-08)

Year	*Unit cost at current prices (in ₹)*	*Percentage increase over the previous year*	*Index of growth*	*Unit cost at constant prices (1993-94 =100)*	*Percentage increase over the previous year*	*Index of growth*
1	2	3	4	5	6	7
1997-98	13760.22	—	100.00	10361.61	—	100.00
1998-99	17567.34	27.67	127.67	12485.67	20.50	120.49
1999-00	21672.94	23.37	157.51	14915.99	19.46	143.95
2000-01	29500.45	36.12	214.39	18946.98	27.02	182.85
2001-02	40992.73	38.96	297.91	25413.97	34.13	245.26
2002-03	48441.46	18.17	352.05	29041.64	14.27	280.27
2003-04	43622.65	–9.95	317.03	24799.69	–14.61	239.33
2004-05	45838.29	5.08	333.13	24473.19	–1.32	236.18
2005-06	43179.95	–5.80	313.81	22075.64	–9.80	213.04
2006-07	57642.57	33.49	418.91	27954.69	26.63	269.78
2007-08	58810.26	2.03	427.40	27264.84	–2.47	263.12
CAGR(%)	14.64			9.24		

Source: Field Survey, 2009.

student public cost at current prices rose from 100 in 1997-98 to 427.40 in 2007-08, and the index of growth of the same at constant prices went up from 100 in 1997-98 to 263.12 in 2007-08. This shows that the state government continuously shouldered larger share of the total cost per unit.

Trend of Public Cost per Unit and Type of Institutions

As seen in Table 5.4, the unit public cost of higher education in general degree colleges has gone up from ₹ 12836.77 in 1997-98 to ₹ 59310.48 in 2007-08, registering an annual compound growth rate of 15.91 per cent at current prices. However, the annual compound growth rate was only 10.45 per cent at constant prices, resulting from an increase in unit cost from ₹ 9666.24 to ₹ 27496.74 during the same period. Wide variations were observed in the annual growth rates, both in current and constant prices, with negative values as well. The index of growth shows that unit cost increased by 362.03 per cent at current prices and by 184.44 per cent at constant prices.

In case of professional colleges (Table 5.5), unit public cost grew at an annual compound rate of 12.85 and 7.54 per cent at current and constant prices, respectively. Annual average growth rate hovered around 26 to 27 per cent for the years 1998-99, 1999-2000 and 2007-08. As for the other years it ranged from a low of (–) 8.92 per cent in 2005-06 to a high of 40.27 per cent in 2002-03. In terms of constant prices the annual average growth rate was negative for as many as three consecutive years starting from 2003-04, and significant variations were observed for the rest of the years. Sharp increase in the index of growth was noticed in current prices from 100 to 386.71 per cent, and in constant prices from 100 to 238.08 per cent during the period 1997-98 to 2007-08.

In Table 5.6, the expenditure profile of technical institutions shows an altogether different trend in the per unit public cost of education. In current prices, the compound annual growth rate was (–) 4.58 per cent and the index of growth is also seen to have fallen down to 91.18 in 2007-08 from 100 in 1997-98. Annual average growth rate markedly varied from year to year. Similarly, at constant prices also the compound annual growth rate was negative at (–) 9.07 per cent, and the index of growth almost halved, falling from

Table 5.4: Per Unit Public Cost of Education in General Degree Colleges (1997-98 to 2007-08)

Year	*Unit cost at current prices (in ₹)*	*Percentage increase over the previous year*	*Index of growth*	*Unit cost at constant prices (1993-94=100)*	*Percentage increase over the previous year*	*Index of growth*
1	2	3	4	5	6	7
1997-98	12836.77	—	100.00	9666.24	—	100.00
1998-99	16454.42	28.18	128.18	11694.68	20.98	120.98
1999-00	20568.15	25.00	160.23	14155.65	21.04	146.43
2000-01	28651.66	39.30	223.20	18401.84	30.00	190.36
2001-02	41931.29	46.35	326.64	25995.84	41.27	268.91
2002-03	50311.87	19.99	391.93	30162.99	16.03	312.02
2003-04	44712.58	–11.13	348.31	25419.32	–15.73	262.95
2004-05	47910.18	7.15	373.22	25579.38	0.63	264.61
2005-06	44520.44	–7.08	346.81	22760.96	–11.02	235.45
2006-07	60057.74	34.90	467.85	29125.96	27.96	301.29
2007-08	59310.48	–1.24	462.03	27496.74	–5.59	284.44
CAGR(%)	**15.91**			**10.45**		

Source: Field Survey, 2009.

Table 5.5: Per Unit Public Cost of Education in Professional Colleges (1997-98 to 2007-08)

Year	*Unit cost at current prices (in ₹)*	*Percentage increase over the previous year*	*Index of growth*	*Unit cost at constant prices (1993-94=100)*	*Percentage increase over the previous year*	*Index of growth*
1	2	3	4	5	6	7
1997-98	12482.76	—	100.00	9399.67	—	100.00
1998-99	15813.41	26.68	126.68	11239.09	19.57	119.56
1999-00	19950.82	26.16	159.82	13730.78	22.17	146.07
2000-01	22384.78	12.20	179.32	14376.86	4.71	152.95
2001-02	27820.57	24.28	222.87	17247.72	19.97	183.49
2002-03	39023.87	40.27	312.62	23395.61	35.64	248.89
2003-04	40474.16	3.72	324.23	23009.76	–1.65	244.78
2004-05	37457.55	–7.45	300.07	19998.69	–13.09	212.75
2005-06	34114.62	-8.92	273.29	17441.01	–12.79	185.54
2006-07	38136.46	11.79	305.51	18494.89	6.04	196.75
2007-08	48272.51	26.58	386.71	22379.47	21.00	238.08
CAGR(%)	12.85			7.54		

Source: Field Survey, 2009.

100 in 1997-98 to 56.14 in 2007-08. The annual growth rates had practically declined for five years ranging from (–) 40.75 per cent to (–) 9.18 per cent and for another five years it ranged between 0.40 per cent and 31.82 per cent.

Table 5.6: Per Unit Public Cost of Education in Technical Institutions (1997-98 to 2007-08)

Year	*Unit cost at current prices (in ₹)*	*Percentage increase over the previous year*	*Index of growth*	*Unit cost at constant prices (1993-94=100)*	*Percentage increase over the previous year*	*Index of growth*
1	2	3	4	5	6	7
1997-98	67905.51	—	100.00	51133.67	—	100.00
1998-99	64161.85	–5.51	94.49	45601.88	–10.82	89.18
1999-00	66522.29	3.68	97.96	45782.72	0.40	89.53
2000-01	75151.52	12.97	110.67	48266.87	5.43	94.39
2001-02	46127.60	–38.62	67.93	28597.39	–40.75	55.93
2002-03	37328.08	–19.08	54.97	22378.95	–21.74	43.77
2003-04	34091.74	–8.67	50.20	19381.32	–13.39	37.90
2004-05	32968.00	–3.30	48.55	17601.71	–9.18	34.42
2005-06	36461.23	10.60	53.69	18640.71	5.90	36.45
2006-07	50666.67	38.96	74.61	24571.61	31.82	48.05
2007-08	61920.08	22.21	91.18	28706.57	16.83	56.14
CAGR (%)	–4.58			–9.07		

Source: Field Survey, 2009.

Off-Putting Cases of Public Cost per Unit

Three abhorrent instances of per unit public cost have been identified below. One is with Technical Institutions and the other two are with Mizoram University and ICFAI University, Mizoram.

Under the impact of Third Technician Education Project of the World Bank the two Polytechnics of Mizoram received a significant amount of soft loan. Accordingly, heavy expenditures were incurred on recurring and non-recurring heads, as seen in Table 5.6(A), under this Externally Aided Project (EAP) during 2001-02 to 2007-08.

Quite high public cost per unit is observed (as high as ₹ 340370.90 in 2001-02) when the expenditures under EAP are added to the regular expenditures during the said period. This is shown in Table 5.6(B).

Table 5.6 (A): Externally Aided Project

Year	*Recurring Cost (In ₹ Lakhs)*	*Non-recurring Cost (In ₹ Lakhs)*	*Total Cost (In ₹ Lakhs)*
2001-02	991.60 (100)	0	991.60 (100)
2002-03	878.06 (100)	0	878.06 (100)
2003-04	359.00 (38.64)	570.00 (61.36)	929.00 (100)
2004-05	584.76 (47.82)	638.00 (52.18)	1222.76 (100)
2005-06	458.00 (53.07)	405.00 (46.93)	863.00 (100)
2006-07	0	0	0
2007-08	49.00 (100)	0	49.00 (100)

Note: Figures in brackets represent percentages.

Source: Field Survey, 2009.

Table 5.6 (B) : Per Unit Public Cost of Technical Education with EAP

Year	*Regular Expenditure (In ₹ Lakhs)*	*EAP Expenditure (In ₹ Lakhs)*	*Total Expenditure (In ₹ Lakhs)*	*Enrolment*	*Unit Cost (In ₹)*
2001-02	155.45	991.60	1147.05	337	340370.90
2002-03	142.22	878.06	1020.28	381	267790.00
2003-04	148.64	929.00	1077.64	436	247165.10
2004-05	164.84	1222.76	1387.60	500	277520.00
2005-06	183.40	863.00	1046.40	503	208031.80
2006-07	243.20	0.00	243.20	480	50666.67
2007-08	317.65	49.00	366.65	513	71471.73

Source: Field Survey, 2009.

Similarly, the atypically high public costs per unit in Mizoram University (ranging from ₹ 245972.57 to ₹ 529820.28 between 2002-03 and 2007-08) and ICFAI University, Mizoram (ranging from ₹ 100600.00 to ₹ 180714.29 between 2005-06 and 2007-08) are provided in Table 5.6(C) and Table 5.6(D), respectively.

Thus, the above three estimates of per unit public cost are treated as statistical out layers in the present study and hence are excluded from the general exercise of calculating public cost per unit of higher education in Mizoram.

Table 5.6 (C): Per Unit Public Cost of Education in Mizoram University

Year	Recurring Cost (In ₹ Lakhs)	Non-recurring Cost (In ₹ Lakhs)	Total Cost (In ₹ Lakhs)	Enrolment	Unit Cost at Current Prices (In ₹)
2002-03	711.96 (72.18)	274.39 (27.82)	986.35 (100)	401	245972.57
2003-04	741.96 (45.63)	883.94 (54.37)	1625.90 (100)	435	373770.11
2004-05	815.48 (37.77)	1343.78 (62.23)	2159.26 (100)	492	438873.98
2005-06	929.15 (30.27)	2140.71 (69.73)	3069.86 (100)	543	565351.75
2006-07	1217.01 (32.16)	2567.57 (67.84)	3784.58 (100)	591	640368.87
2007-08	2190.41 (63.51)	1258.72 (36.49)	3449.13 (100)	651	529820.28

Note: Figures in brackets represent percentages.

Source: Field Survey, 2009.

Table 5.6 (D): Per Unit Public Cost of Education in ICFAI University

Year	Recurring Cost (In ₹ Lakhs)	Non-recurring Cost (In ₹ Lakhs)	Total Cost (In ₹ Lakhs)	Enrolment	Unit Cost at Current Prices (In ₹)
)05-06	15.18 (50.30)	15.00 (49.70)	30.18 (100)	30	100600.00
)06-07	69.21 (82.19)	15.00 (17.81)	84.21 (100)	140	60150.00
)07-08	147.50 (38.87)	232.00 (61.13)	379.50 (100)	210	180714.29

Note: Figures in brackets represent percentages.

Source: Field Survey, 2009.

Recurring and Non-Recurring Expenditure on Higher Education

In Mizoram, public educational expenditure on recurring heads had increased from ₹ 884.12 lakhs in 1997-98 to ₹ 3382.98 lakhs in 2007-08 at current prices, registering a growth rate of 13.92 per cent per annum. Non-recurring expenditure, however, grew at an annual compound growth rate of only 10.24 per cent, i.e. from ₹ 125.88 lakhs in 1997-98 to ₹ 376.76 lakhs in 2007-08. Of the total educational outlay recurring expenditure claims the lion's share ranging from 84.56 to 91.88 per cent leaving only 8.12 to 15.44 per cent for non-recurring heads during the period under study (Table 5.7). In real

Table 5.7: Recurring and Non-Recurring Expenditure on Higher Education in Mizoram (at Current Prices)

(In ₹ Lakhs)

Year	*Recurring*	*%*	*Non-recurring*	*%*	*Total*
1997-98	884.12	87.54	125.88	12.46	1010.00
1998-99	1061.57	85.13	185.36	14.87	1246.93
1999-00	1159.34	84.56	211.69	15.44	1371.03
2000-01	1413.31	86.37	223.08	13.63	1636.39
2001-02	2939.21	91.88	259.64	8.12	3198.85
2002-03	2090.85	87.73	292.47	12.27	2383.32
2003-04	2158.87	89.53	252.59	10.47	2411.46
2004-05	2377.02	90.27	256.21	9.73	2633.41
2005-06	2624.55	87.43	377.32	12.57	3001.87
2006-07	3225.84	88.51	418.09	11.49	3644.74
2007-08	3382.98	89.98	376.76	10.02	3759.74
CAGR	13.92		10.24		13.45

Source: Field Survey, 2009.

Table 5.8: Recurring and Non-Recurring Expenditure on Higher Education in Mizoram (at Constant Prices)

(In ₹ Lakhs)

Year	*Recurring*	*Non-recurring*	*Total*
1997-98	665.75	94.79	760.54
1998-99	754.49	131.74	886.23
1999-00	797.89	145.69	943.59
2000-01	907.71	143.28	1050.99
2001-02	1822.20	160.97	1983.17
2002-03	1253.51	175.34	1428.85
2003-04	1227.33	143.60	1370.93
2004-05	1269.19	136.79	1405.99
2005-06	1341.79	192.90	1534.70
2006-07	1564.42	203.15	1767.58
2007-08	1568.37	174.67	1743.04
CAGR	8.56	5.05	8.11

Source: Field Survey, 2009

terms, the compound annual growth rates of recurring and non-recurring expenditure were 8.56 and 5.05 per cent, respectively, during the same period (Table 5.8).

Recurring and Non-Recurring Expenditure and Type of Institutions

The estimates of recurring and non-recurring expenditure of higher education for the three types of educational institutions are presented (i) at current prices in Table 5.9, and (ii) at constant prices in Table 5.10.

In case of general degree colleges, the annual compound growth rate of total public expenditure was 13.84 per cent as the outlay increased from ₹ 847.74 lakhs in 1997-98 to ₹ 3243.69 lakhs in 2007-08. Of the total expenditure, 85.27 to 90.13 per cent were spent on recurring and 9.87 to 14.73 per cent on non-recurring heads. The growth rates of recurring and non-recurring expenditure were 14.09 and 12.06 per cent per annum, respectively.

Public expenditure grew at an annual compound growth rate of 10.81 per cent in case of professional colleges. It was ₹ 76.02 lakhs in 1997-98 and stood at ₹ 198.40 lakhs in 2007-08. Share of recurring expenditure ranged from 72.61 per cent at the minimum to 83.07 per cent at the maximum. Non-recurring expenditure claimed only 16.93 to 27.39 per cent of the total public expenditure during the same period.

Trend of recurring and non-recurring expenditure on technical institutions shows a different picture. Recurring expenditure had been continually increasing from ₹ 68.83 lakhs in 1997-98 to ₹ 317.65 lakhs in 2007-08, except the reversals in 1999-2000 and 2002-03. The growth rate of recurring expenditure was calculated to be 14.89 per cent per annum. As to the non-recurring expenditure, it was incurred up to the year 2002-03. This may be due to the heavy expenditure incurred under the "Third Technician Education Project" of World Bank, 2001-2007. Non-recurring expenditure increased from ₹ 17.41 lakhs in 1997-98 to ₹ 24.5 lakhs in 1998-99, but fell down to ₹ 22.69 lakhs in 1999-00. It reached the maximum amount at ₹ 26.72 lakhs in 2000-2001, then declined to ₹ 8.55 lakhs in 2001-02 and finally, to the least at ₹ 7.55 lakhs in 2002-03. Thus the compound annual growth rate was estimated to be (-)18.53 per cent. However,

Table 5.9: Recurring and Non-Recurring Expenditure of Higher Educational Institutions (at Current Prices)

(In ₹ Lakhs)

General Degree Colleges	*Recurring*	*Percentage*	*Non-recurring*	*Percentage*	*Total*
1997-98	752.54	88.77	95.02	11.23	847.74
1998-99	906.54	86.45	142.10	13.55	1048.64
1999-00	1017.76	85.27	175.81	14.73	1193.57
2000-01	1229.85	87.44	176.66	12.56	1406.51
2001-02	2686.69	88.02	229.57	11.98	2916.26
2002-03	1836.00	87.68	257.98	12.32	2093.98
2003-04	1903.06	89.36	226.60	10.64	2129.66
2004-05	2081.78	90.13	227.97	9.87	2309.75
2005-06	2300.57	86.95	345.28	13.05	2645.85
2006-07	2837.58	88.28	376.71	11.72	3214.29
2007-08	2921.27	90.06	322.42	9.94	3243.69
CAGR	14.09		12.06		13.84
Professional Colleges	*Recurring*	*Percentage*	*Non-recurring*	*Percentage*	*Total*
1997-98	62.75	82.55	13.27	17.45	76.02
1998-99	68.53	78.51	18.76	21.49	87.29
1999-00	59.83	81.94	13.19	18.06	73.02
2000-01	86.18	81.39	19.07	18.61	105.88
2001-02	105.62	83.07	21.52	16.93	127.14
2002-03	120.18	81.69	26.94	18.31	147.12
2003-04	107.17	80.48	25.99	19.52	133.16
2004-05	130.58	82.22	28.24	17.78	158.82
2005-06	140.58	81.44	32.04	18.56	172.62
2006-07	145.06	77.47	42.19	22.53	187.25
2007-08	144.06	72.61	54.34	27.39	198.04
CAGR	10.08		13.43		10.81
Technical Institutions	*Recurring*	*Percentage*	*Non-recurring*	*Percentage*	*Total*
1997-98	68.83	79.81	17.41	20.19	86.24
1998-99	86.05	77.93	24.05	22.07	111.00
1999-00	81.75	78.27	22.69	21.73	104.44
2000-01	97.28	78.45	26.72	21.55	124.00
2001-02	146.09	94.50	8.55	5.50	155.45
2002-03	134.67	94.69	7.55	5.31	142.22
2003-04	148.64	100.00	0	0	148.64
2004-05	164.84	100.00	0	0	164.84
2005-06	183.04	100.00	0	0	183.40
2006-07	243.02	100.00	0	0	243.20
2007-08	317.65	100.00	0	0	317.65
CAGR	14.89		–18.53		11.39

Table 5.10 : Recurring and Non-Recurring Expenditure of Higher Educational Institutions (at Constant Prices)

(In ₹ Lakhs)

General Degree Colleges	*Recurring*	*Non-recurring*	*Total*
1997-98	566.67	71.69	638.36
1998-99	644.31	101.00	745.30
1999-00	700.45	121.00	821.45
2000-01	789.88	113.46	903.35
2001-02	1665.65	142.32	1188.01
2002-03	1100.72	154.66	1255.38
2003-04	1081.90	128.82	1210.72
2004-05	1111.47	121.71	1233.18
2005-06	1176.16	176.52	1352.68
2006-07	1376.13	182.69	1558.82
2007-08	1354.32	149.48	1503.80
CAGR	8.72	6.78	8.90
Professional Colleges	*Recurring*	*Non-recurring*	*Total*
1997-98	48.42	10.23	58.65
1998-99	48.05	13.16	61.21
1999-00	42.22	18.82	61.03
2000-01	59.19	13.53	72.72
2001-02	70.09	14.29	84.38
2002-03	74.12	16.61	90.74
2003-04	65.55	15.90	81.46
2004-05	75.44	16.33	91.76
2005-06	79.02	18.01	97.03
2006-07	75.04	21.82	96.86
2007-08	82.56	31.15	113.70
CAGR	6.33	7.49	6.54
Technical Institutions	*Recurring*	*Non-recurring*	*Total*
1997-98	51.83	13.11	64.94
1998-99	61.48	17.41	78.89
1999-00	56.26	15.62	71.88
2000-01	62.48	17.16	79.64
2001-02	91.07	5.30	96.37
2002-03	80.74	4.53	85.26
2003-04	84.50	0	84.50
2004-05	88.01	0	88.01
2005-06	93.76	0	93.76
2006-07	117.94	0	117.94
2007-08	147.26	0	147.26
CAGR	9.49	–22.21	6.15

Source: Field Survey, 2009.

total public expenditure on technical institutions grew at the rate of 11.39 per cent per annum, i.e. from ₹ 86.24 lakhs in 1997-98 to ₹ 317.65 lakhs in 2007-08. Share of recurring expenditure was 77.93 to 94.69 per cent between 1997-98 and 2002-03, while it was 100 per cent from 2003-04 to 2007-08, as there was no non-recurring expenditure during this period. As a consequence, non-recurring expenditure constituted only 5.31 to 22.07 per cent of the total public expenditure during 1997-98 to 2002-03.

At constant prices, the growth rates of both recurring and non-recurring expenditure were lower than at current prices. In absolute terms, recurring expenditure increased by ₹ 787.65 lakhs and non-recurring expenditure by ₹ 77.79 lakhs for general degree colleges during the period 1997-98 to 2007-08. In case of professional colleges the absolute increase was ₹ 34.14 lakhs and ₹ 20.92 lakhs, respectively in recurring and non-recurring expenditures during the same period. Finally, ₹ 95.43 lakhs was estimated to be the absolute increase in recurring expenditure of technical institutions during 1997-98 to 2007-08. Non-recurring expenditure, however, declined by ₹ 8.58 lakhs in absolute terms, during the period 1997-98 to 2002-03.

Composition and Trend of Recurring Expenditure

The itemization of recurring cost in general degree colleges, professional colleges and technical institutions is presented in the following section.

Composition of Recurring Cost in General Degree Colleges

Table 5.11 reveals that, in the year 1997-98 salary component accounts for 91.03 per cent (₹ 685.04 lakhs) of the total recurring cost (₹ 752.54 lakhs). This percentage share stood at 89.05 per cent (₹ 2601.39 lakhs) of the total (₹ 2921.27 lakhs) in 2007-08, registering a growth rate of 14.03 per cent per annum. However, in real terms, salary component grew at an annual compound growth rate of 8.67 per cent only (Table 5.12). The second largest head of expenditure is scholarship, which claims 2.55 per cent to 6.60 per cent of the total recurring expenditure during the period 1997-98 to 2007-08. During the same period, each of the items like, maintenance of building, furniture, expenditure on

Table 5.11: Composition and Trend of Recurring Cost in General Degree Colleges (at Current Prices)

(In ₹ Lakhs)

Items	Salary, DA etc.	Building (repaires etc.)	Furniture	Library	Scholar-ship	Labora-tory	Student activities	Telephone/ Internet	Travelling allowances	Other Costs	Total
1997-98	685.04	0.98	1.66	7.68	26.41	4.14	5.64	4.59	3.09	13.32	752.54
	(91.03)	(0.13)	(0.22)	(1.02)	(3.51)	(0.55)	(0.75)	(0.61)	(0.41)	(1.77)	
1998-99	815.07	5.80	8.61	7.98	25.84	2.81	7.52	5.26	2.09	25.56	906.54
	(89.91)	(0.64)	(0.95)	(0.88)	(2.85)	(0.31)	(0.83)	(0.58)	(0.23)	(2.82)	
1999-00	939.90	1.83	1.73	7.73	33.79	0.81	11.40	7.43	1.63	11.50	1017.76
	(92.35)	(0.18)	(0.17)	(0.76)	(3.32)	(0.08)	(1.12)	(0.73)	(0.16)	(1.13)	
2000-01	1123.47	3.81	2.83	3.94	46.00	2.34	6.89	10.95	4.67	24.97	1229.85
	(91.35)	(0.31)	(0.23)	(0.32)	(3.74)	(0.19)	(0.56)	(0.89)	(0.38)	(2.03)	
2001-02	2392.77	11.82	3.49	22.30	118.75	15.58	20.42	25.52	11.28	64.75	2686.69
	(89.06)	(0.44)	(0.13)	(0.83)	(4.42)	(0.58)	(0.76)	(0.95)	(0.42)	(2.41)	
2002-03	1726.39	6.79	3.30	10.10	46.82	5.32	13.22	15.24	2.20	6.61	1836.00
	(94.03)	(0.37)	(0.18)	(0.55)	(2.55)	(0.29)	(0.72)	(0.83)	(0.12)	(0.36)	
2003-04	1783.55	4.38	2.09	11.61	57.28	4.00	5.52	14.84	5.14	14.65	1903.06
	(93.72)	(0.23)	(0.11)	(0.61)	(3.01)	(0.21)	(0.29)	(0.78)	(0.27)	(0.77)	
2004-05	1910.24	7.49	5.41	11.87	76.40	8.74	12.91	25.40	10.83	12.49	2081.78
	(91.76)	(0.36)	(0.26)	(0.57)	(3.67)	(0.42)	(0.62)	(1.22)	(0.52)	(0.60)	
2005-06	2131.25	9.43	1.84	15.64	80.06	5.06	21.17	22.32	5.75	8.05	2300.57
	(92.64)	(0.41)	(0.08)	(0.68)	(3.48)	(0.22)	(0.92)	(0.97)	(0.25)	(0.35)	
2006-07	2542.19	6.24	3.41	11.07	147.84	4.82	21.85	37.17	10.50	52.50	2837.58
	(89.59)	(0.22)	(0.12)	(0.39)	(5.21)	(0.17)	(0.77)	(1.31)	(0.37)	(1.85)	
2007-08	2601.39	11.39	1.75	26.88	192.80	18.11	19.57	30.67	8.18	10.52	2921.27
	(89.05)	(0.39)	(0.06)	(0.92)	(6.6)	(0.62)	(0.67)	(1.05)	(0.28)	(0.36)	
Growth Rates %	14.03	17.6	-2.22	10.76	19.71	15.98	11.82	21.87	15.66	–2.02	14.09

Note: Figures in the parentheses represent percentages.

Source: Field Survey, 2009.

Table 5.12: Composition and Trend of Recurring Cost in General Degree Colleges (At Constant Prices)

(In ₹ Lakhs)

Items	*Salary, DA etc*	*Building (repaires etc)*	*Furniture*	*Library*	*Scholarship*	*Laboratory*	*Student activities*	*Telephone/ internet*	*Travelling allowances*	*Other costs*	*Total*
1997-98	515.84	0.74	1.25	5.78	19.89	3.12	4.25	3.46	2.32	10.03	566.67
1998-99	579.30	4.12	6.12	5.67	18.36	2.00	5.35	3.74	1.48	18.17	644.31
1999-00	646.87	1.26	1.19	5.32	23.26	0.56	7.85	5.11	1.12	7.92	700.45
2000-01	721.56	2.45	1.82	2.53	29.54	1.50	4.42	7.03	3.00	16.03	789.88
2001-02	1483.43	7.33	2.17	13.82	73.62	9.66	12.66	15.82	7.00	40.14	1665.65
2002-03	1035.01	4.07	1.98	6.05	28.07	3.19	7.93	9.14	1.32	3.96	1100.72
2003-04	1013.96	2.49	1.19	6.60	32.57	2.27	3.14	8.44	2.92	8.33	1081.90
2004-05	1019.88	4.00	2.89	6.34	40.79	4.67	6.89	13.56	5.78	6.67	1111.47
2005-06	1089.60	4.82	0.94	8.00	40.93	2.59	10.82	11.41	2.94	4.12	1176.16
2006-07	1232.87	3.03	1.65	5.37	71.70	2.34	10.60	18.03	5.09	25.46	1376.13
2007-08	1206.02	5.28	0.81	12.46	89.39	8.40	9.07	14.22	3.79	4.88	1354.32
Growth rates %	8.67	12.08	-6.81	5.55	14.08	10.52	6.56	16.14	10.23	–6.63	8.72

Source: Field Survey, 2009

laboratory and travelling allowances claimed less than 1 per cent of the total recurring cost, while library accounted for 1.02 per cent in 1997-98 and student activities accounted for 1.12 per cent of the total in 1999-2000. The percentage share of telephone/internet cost shows an upward trend in the recent years, i.e. 1.22, 1.31 and 1.05 per cent in 2004-05, 2006-07 and 2007-08, respectively. The growth rates of expenditure per annum on all the items (negative in case of furniture and other stuff) at current prices were higher than those at constant prices. This means that, real expenditure grew at a slower pace. The total recurring cost, at constant prices, had increased 2.39 times, from ₹ 566.67 lakhs in 1997-98 to ₹ 1354.32 lakhs in 2007-08, registering an annual compound growth rate of 8.72 per cent.

Composition of Recurring Cost in Professional Colleges

The composition of recurring cost in professional colleges at current prices is presented in Table 5.13 and at constant prices in Table 5.14. Here, also the pattern of highest expenditure on salary (78.94 to 90 per cent of the total) followed by Scholarship (4.46 to 16.63 per cent of the total) is observed during the period between 1997-98 and 2007-08. The annual growth rates of salary and scholarship were 19.41 and 10.82 per cent, respectively. Other components claim a very nominal share of recurring expenditure, the highest being 1.45 per cent of the total (₹ 1.89 lakhs) in case of library during the same period. While the growth rate of all the items were positive at current prices, it grew at a negative rate (–2.54%) in case of laboratory at constant prices.

Composition of Recurring Cost in Technical Institutions

From Table 5.15 it is evident that, salary component of technical institutions continues to claim the lion's share, ranging from a low of 87.52 to a high of 91.21 per cent during the period 1997-98 to 2007-08. Although scholarship occupies the second position, the percentage shares decreases considerably for the whole period under study, with the highest percentage being 3.23 of the total recurring cost in the year 2001-02. The highest growth rate was recorded at 27.75 per cent per annum in case of maintenance of buildings and the least rate

Table 5.13: Composition and Trend of Recurring Cost in Professional Colleges (at Current Prices)

(In ₹ Lakhs)

Items	Salary, DA etc.	Building (repaires etc.)	Fur-niture	Library	Scholar-ship	Laboratory/ Equipments	Student activities	Telephone/ Internet	Travelling allowances	Other Costs	Total
1997-98	54.61 (87.02)	0.35 (0.56)	0.48 (0.76)	0.48 (0.76)	4.16 (6.63)	0.56 (0.89)	0.51 (0.82)	0.38 (0.61)	0.58 (0.93)	0.64 (1.02)	62.75
1998-99	60.32 (88.02)	0.32 (0.47)	0.24 (0.35)	0.47 (0.68)	4.95 (7.22)	0.67 (0.98)	0.51 (0.75)	0.27 (0.39)	0.28 (0.41)	0.50 (0.73)	68.53
1999-00	53.40 (89.26)	0.44 (0.73)	0.16 (0.26)	0.54 (0.91)	2.67 (4.46)	0.26 (0.44)	0.45 (0.76)	0.31 (0.52)	0.23 (0.38)	1.36 (2.28)	59.83
2000-01	77.56 (90.00)	0.33 (0.38)	0.35 (0.41)	0.75 (0.87)	4.41 (5.12)	0.53 (0.61)	0.72 (0.83)	0.61 (0.71)	0.39 (0.45)	0.53 (0.62)	86.18
2001-02	92.08 (87.18)	0.64 (0.61)	0.50 (0.47)	1.31 (1.24)	5.34 (5.06)	0.82 (0.78)	0.64 (0.61)	0.52 (0.49)	0.88 (0.83)	2.88 (2.73)	105.62
2002-03	106.15 (88.33)	0.59 (0.49)	0.35 (0.29)	0.66 (0.55)	7.22 (6.01)	0.61 (0.51)	0.65 (0.54)	0.81 (0.67)	0.61 (0.51)	2.52 (2.10)	120.18
2003-04	93.01 (86.79)	0.87 (0.81)	0.55 (0.51)	0.90 (0.84)	8.60 (8.02)	0.28 (0.26)	0.79 (0.74)	0.51 (0.48)	0.53 (0.49)	1.14 (1.06)	107.17
2004-05	113.57 (86.97)	0.69 (0.53)	0.34 (0.26)	1.89 (1.45)	8.27 (6.33)	0.63 (0.48)	0.76 (0.58)	1.46 (1.12)	0.82 (0.63)	2.15 (1.65)	130.58
2005-06	122.70 (87.28)	0.41 (0.29)	1.01 (0.72)	0.67 (0.48)	7.62 (5.42)	0.59 (0.42)	1.14 (0.81)	1.38 (0.98)	0.52 (0.37)	4.54 (3.23)	140.58
2006-07	126.39 (87.13)	1.09 (0.75)	0.65 (0.45)	0.83 (0.57)	9.50 (6.55)	0.57 (0.39)	1.33 (0.92)	1.91 (1.32)	0.62 (0.43)	2.16 (1.49)	145.06
2007-08	113.72 (78.94)	0.92 (0.64)	0.46 (0.32)	[illegible] (0.65)	23.96 (16.63)	0.75 (0.52)	1.05 (0.73)	0.88 (0.61)	0.76 (0.53)	0.62 (0.43)	144.06
Growth Rates %	19.41	10.82	8.86	7.30	15.91	2.34	10.07	18.03	7.5	10.7	10.08

Note: Figures in the parentheses represent percentages.

Source: Field Survey, 2009.

Table 5.14: Composition and Trend of Recurring Cost in Professional Colleges (at Constant Prices)

(in ₹ Lakhs)

Items	Salary, DA etc	Building (repaires etc)	Furniture	Library	Scholar-ship	Laboratory	Student activities	Telephone/ internet	Travelling allowances	Other costs	Total
1997-98	41.12	0.26	0.36	0.36	3.13	0.42	0.39	0.29	0.44	0.48	47.25
1998-99	42.87	0.23	0.17	0.33	3.52	0.48	0.37	0.19	0.20	0.36	48.71
1999-00	36.75	0.30	0.11	0.37	1.84	0.18	0.31	0.21	0.16	0.94	41.18
2000-01	49.82	0.21	0.23	0.48	2.83	0.34	0.46	0.39	0.25	0.34	55.35
2001-02	57.09	0.40	0.31	0.81	3.31	0.51	0.40	0.32	0.54	1.79	65.48
2002-03	63.64	0.35	0.21	0.40	4.33	0.37	0.39	0.48	0.37	1.51	72.05
2003-04	52.88	0.49	0.31	0.51	4.89	0.16	0.45	0.29	0.30	0.65	60.93
2004-05	60.63	0.37	0.18	1.01	4.41	0.33	0.40	0.78	0.44	1.15	69.72
2005-06	62.73	0.21	0.52	0.34	3.90	0.30	0.58	0.70	0.27	2.32	71.87
2006-07	61.30	0.53	0.32	0.40	4.61	0.27	0.65	0.93	0.30	1.05	70.35
2007-08	52.72	0.43	0.21	0.43	11.11	0.35	0.49	0.41	0.35	0.29	66.79
Growth Rates %	4.26	5.58	3.86	2.29	10.46	-2.54	4.81	12.47	2.49	5.46	4.90

Source: Field Survey, 2009

Table 5.15: Composition and Trend of Recurring Expenditure (at Current Prices)

(In ₹ Lakhs)

Items	Salary, DA etc.	Building (repaires etc.)	Furniture	Library	Scholar-ship	Laboratory/ Equipments	Student activities	Telephone/ Internet	Travelling allowances	Other Costs	Total
1997-98	61.20	0.38	0.33	0.43	1.70	1.22	0.24	0.30	0.45	2.59	68.83
	(88.91)	(0.55)	(0.48)	(0.63)	(2.47)	(1.77)	(0.35)	(0.43)	(0.65)	(3.76)	
1998-99	77.18	0.33	0.49	0.48	2.60	0.80	0.36	0.44	0.51	3.29	86.50
	(89.23)	(0.38)	(0.57)	(0.56)	(3.01)	(0.93)	(0.42)	(0.51)	(0.59)	(3.80)	
1999-00	73.60	0.34	0.27	0.39	2.35	0.72	0.42	0.43	0.40	2.84	81.75
	(90.03)	(0.41)	(0.33)	(0.48)	(2.87)	(0.88)	(0.51)	(0.52)	(0.49)	(3.48)	
2000-01	86.90	0.60	0.45	0.59	2.36	0.74	0.37	0.55	0.69	4.02	97.28
	(89.33)	(0.62)	(0.46)	(0.61)	(2.43)	(0.76)	(0.38)	(0.57)	(0.71)	(4.13)	
2001-02	130.09	0.78	0.78	0.62	4.74	1.51	0.69	1.06	0.93	5.70	146.90
	(88.56)	(0.53)	(0.53)	(0.42)	(3.23)	(1.03)	(0.47)	(0.72)	(0.63)	(3.88)	
2002-03	122.83	0.61	1.17	0.47	3.11	1.17	0.39	0.93	0.92	3.07	134.67
	(91.21)	(0.45)	(0.87)	(0.35)	(2.31)	(0.87)	(0.29)	(0.69)	(0.68)	(2.28)	
2003-04	130.09	1.58	1.37	0.79	4.50	1.10	0.64	1.25	0.80	6.53	148.64
	(87.52)	(1.06)	(0.92)	(0.53)	(3.03)	(0.74)	(0.43)	(0.84)	(0.54)	(4.39)	
2004-05	146.46	1.57	1.20	1.07	4.02	2.18	0.61	1.05	0.71	5.97	164.84
	(88.85)	(0.95)	(0.73)	(0.65)	(2.44)	(1.32)	(0.37)	(0.64)	(0.43)	(3.62)	
2005-06	161.30	3.25	1.63	0.90	4.36	1.52	0.94	1.08	0.95	7.46	183.40
	(87.95)	(1.77)	(0.89)	(0.49)	(2.38)	(0.83)	(0.51)	(0.59)	(0.52)	(4.07)	
2006-07	220.63	2.07	1.24	1.53	6.20	2.55	1.12	1.63	0.78	5.45	243.20
	(90.72)	(0.85)	(0.51)	(0.63)	(2.55)	(1.05)	(0.46)	(0.67)	(0.32)	(2.24)	
2007-08	286.17	2.92	1.46	1.43	5.11	3.08	1.37	2.29	2.38	11.44	317.65
	(90.09)	(0.92)	(0.46)	(0.45)	(1.61)	(0.97)	(0.43)	(0.72)	(0.75)	(3.6)	
Growth Rates %	14.93	27.75	18.93	14.18	11.37	12.91	16.28	19.53	12.06	12.82	14.89

Note: Figures in the parentheses represent percentages.

Source: Field Survey, 2009.

Table 5.16: Composition and Trend of Recurring Cost in Technical Institutions (At Constant Prices)

(In ₹ Lakhs)

Items	*Salary, DA etc.*	*Building (repaires etc.)*	*Furniture*	*Library*	*Scholar-ship*	*Laboratory*	*Student activities*	*Tele-phone/ internet*	*Travelling allowances*	*Other costs*	*Total*
1997-98	46.08	0.29	0.25	0.33	1.28	0.92	0.18	0.22	0.34	1.95	51.83
1998-99	54.86	0.23	0.35	0.34	1.85	0.57	0.26	0.31	0.36	2.34	61.48
1999-00	50.65	0.23	0.19	0.27	1.61	0.50	0.29	0.29	0.28	1.96	56.26
2000-01	55.81	0.39	0.29	0.38	1.52	0.47	0.24	0.36	0.44	2.58	62.48
2001-02	80.65	0.48	0.48	0.38	2.94	0.94	0.43	0.66	0.57	3.53	91.07
2002-03	73.64	0.36	0.70	0.28	1.87	0.70	0.23	0.56	0.55	1.84	80.74
2003-04	73.96	0.90	0.78	0.45	2.56	0.63	0.36	0.71	0.46	3.71	84.50
2004-05	78.20	0.84	0.64	0.57	2.15	1.16	0.33	0.56	0.38	3.19	88.01
2005-06	82.46	1.66	0.83	0.46	2.23	0.78	0.48	0.55	0.49	3.82	93.76
2006-07	107.00	1.00	0.60	0.74	3.01	1.24	0.54	0.79	0.38	2.64	117.94
2007-08	132.67	1.35	0.68	0.66	2.37	1.43	0.63	1.06	1.10	5.30	147.26
Growth Rates %	9.53	21.80	13.33	8.70	6.13	7.59	10.74	13.99	6.82	7.51	9.49

Source: Field Survey, 2009.

was estimated at 11.37 per cent annually in case of scholarship during the same period. However, in real terms (Table 5.16), the highest growth rate was calculated to be 21.80 per cent per annum for repairing expenses of buildings and the least annual growth rate was found to be 6.13 per cent for scholarship.

Composition and Trend of Non-Recurring Expenditure

In the succeeding section, non-recurring expenditure with its components in general degree colleges, professional colleges and technical institutions is analyzed. The itemization shows that some of the heads appear on both sides (recurring and non-recurring) indicating that creation of assets or new additions is of non-recurring type and maintenance is of recurring nature.

Composition of Non-Recurring Cost in General Degree Colleges

In general, among the non-recurring cost components in general degree colleges furniture claims the highest share and equipments the least of the total (Table 5.17). Expenditure on equipments constitutes only 9.87 per cent (₹ 17.44 lakhs) of the total non-recurring cost (₹ 176.66 lakhs) in the year 2000-01, while furniture accounts for 34.05 per cent (₹ 77.62 lakhs) of the total non-recurring expenses (₹ 227.97 lakhs) in 2004-05. During the period 1997-98 to 2007-08, expenditure on furniture recorded the highest annual growth rate (16.02%), followed by equipment (14.77%), library (14.53%) and construction (12.77%). However, at constant prices (Table 5.18), the compound annual growth rates of non-recurring costs on library, construction, equipment and furniture were 9.17, 7.50, 9.38 and 10.59 per cent, respectively.

Composition of Non-Recurring Cost in Professional Colleges

As is revealed in Table 5.19, equipment cost continues to constitute the smallest share of non-recurring cost. It grew from ₹ 2.09 lakhs in 1997-98 to ₹ 8.65 lakhs in 2007-08, i.e. at the rate of 13.10 per cent per annum. As to the other items, library claims 17.42 to 29.36 per

Table 5.17 : Composition and Trend of Non-Recurring Cost in General Degree Colleges (At Current Prices)

(In ₹ Lakhs)

Items	*Library*	*Construction*	*Equipment*	*Furniture*	*Other expenditure*	*Total*
1997-98	13.27 (13.94)	27.18 (28.55)	12.13 (12.74)	25.75 (27.05)	16.87 (17.72)	95.20
1998-99	30.81 (21.68)	22.28 (15.68)	22.95 (16.15)	32.02 (22.53)	34.05 (23.96)	142.10
1999-00	32.03 (18.22)	22.82 (12.98)	24.23 (13.78)	32.67 (18.58)	64.07 (36.44)	175.81
2000-01	48.67 (27.55)	34.54 (19.55)	17.44 (9.87)	45.24 (25.61)	30.77 (17.42)	176.66
2001-02	57.53 (25.06)	71.30 (31.06)	29.52 (12.86)	65.54 (28.55)	5.67 (2.47)	229.57
2002-03	42.44 (16.45)	67.90 (26.32)	30.80 (11.94)	69.06 (26.77)	47.78 (18.52)	257.98
2003-04	46.63 (20.58)	50.69 (22.37)	43.08 (19.01)	70.74 (31.22)	15.45 (6.82)	226.60
2004-05	60.94 (26.73)	40.97 (17.97)	37.77 (16.57)	77.62 (34.05)	10.67 (4.68)	227.97
2005-06	108.49 (31.42)	82.42 (23.87)	49.27 (14.27)	93.99 (27.22)	11.12 (3.22)	345.28
2006-07	89.54 (23.77)	69.35 (18.41)	52.66 (13.98)	121.00 (32.12)	44.15 (11.72)	376.71
2007-08	51.23 (15.89)	71.35 (22.13)	57.49 (17.83)	98.37 (30.51)	43.98 (13.64)	322.42
Growth Rates %	14.53	12.77	14.77	16.02	–0.49	12.06

Note: Figures in the parentheses represent percentages.

Source: Field Survey, 2009.

cent, construction constitutes 14.85 to 31.22 per cent and furniture cost ranges between 13.71 per cent and 30.47 per cent of the total non-recurring cost. In real terms (Table 5.20), construction cost increased marginally from ₹ 3.12 lakhs in 1997-98 to ₹ 3.74 lakhs in 2007-08, registering an annual growth rate of 2.66 per cent. The highest growth rate was observed at 8.69 per cent per annum in case of expenditure on library. Cost of equipment and furniture grew at 7.78 and 3.91 per cent, respectively, during the same period.

Table 5.18: Composition and Trend of Non-Recurring Cost in General Degree Colleges (at Constant Prices)

(In ₹ Lakhs)

Items	Library	Construction	Equip-ment	Furniture	Other expenditure	Total
1997-98	9.99	20.47	9.13	19.39	12.70	71.69
1998-99	21.90	15.84	16.31	22.75	24.20	101.00
1999-00	22.05	15.71	16.67	22.48	44.09	121.00
2000-01	31.26	22.18	11.20	29.06	19.77	113.46
2001-02	35.67	44.21	18.30	40.63	3.52	142.32
2002-03	25.44	40.71	18.47	41.40	28.64	154.66
2003-04	26.51	28.82	24.49	40.22	8.79	128.82
2004-05	32.53	21.87	20.17	41.44	5.70	121.71
2005-06	55.46	42.14	25.19	48.05	5.68	176.52
2006-07	43.43	33.63	25.54	58.68	21.41	182.69
2007-08	23.75	33.08	26.65	45.61	20.39	149.48
Growth Rates %	9.17	7.50	9.38	10.59	–5.21	6.77

Source: Field Survey, 2009

Composition of Non-Recurring Cost in Technical Institutions

The breakup of non-recurring cost in technical institutions for the period 1997-98 to 2002-03 is provided in Table 5.21 at current prices and in Table 5.22 at constant prices. Percentage share of expenditures on library ranged between 15.71 and 27.25 per cent, on construction between 16.83 and 30.15 per cent, on equipment between 16.93 and 32.56 per cent, and on furniture between 11.48 and 21.08 per cent of the total cost, during the same period. The annual growth rates of non-recurring expenditure on all the items were negative both in nominal and in real terms. Total non-recurring cost rose to ₹ 24.50 lakhs in 1998-99 from ₹ 17.41 lakhs in 1997-98, then it fell down to ₹ 22.69 lakhs in 1999-2000. It increased to the highest amount of ₹ 26.72 lakhs in 2000-01, then declined sharply to ₹ 8.55 lakhs and finally to ₹ 7.55 lakhs in 2001-02 and 2002-03, respectively. This trend of total cost results into an annual growth rate of (–)18.53 per cent in nominal terms and (–) 22.21 per cent in real terms.

Table 5.19: Composition and Trend of Non-Recurring Cost in Professional Colleges (At Current Prices)

(In ₹ Lakhs)

Items	*Library*	*Construction*	*Equipment*	*Furniture*	*Other expenditure*	*Total*
1997-98	2.84 (21.43)	4.14 (31.22)	2.09 (15.78)	3.15 (23.76)	1.04 (7.81)	13.27
1998-99	3.72 (19.85)	4.97 (26.51)	2.36 (12.56)	5.72 (30.47)	1.99 (10.61)	18.76
1999-00	2.44 (18.51)	3.12 (23.68)	2.36 (17.87)	2.97 (22.55)	2.29 (17.39)	13.19
2000-01	5.45 (27.67)	3.73 (18.95)	3.30 (16.75)	5.26 (26.68)	1.96 (9.95)	19.7
2001-02	5.28 (24.55)	6.17 (28.68)	4.59 (21.32)	3.31 (15.38)	2.17 (10.07)	21.52
2002-03	6.30 (27.33)	5.61 (24.33)	4.33 (18.78)	5.91 (25.66)	0.90 (3.9)	23.04
2003-04	7.63 (29.36)	5.06 (19.45)	3.80 (14.62)	5.06 (19.45)	4.45 (17.12)	25.99
2004-05	6.86 (24.29)	5.73 (20.3)	3.90 (13.82)	3.95 (13.97)	7.80 (27.62)	28.24
2005-06	5.58 (17.42)	7.94 (24.78)	3.71 (11.59)	8.21 (25.61)	6.60 (20.6)	32.04
2006-07	8.27 (19.59)	7.05 (16.72)	8.11 (19.22)	5.78 (13.71)	12.98 (30.76)	42.19
2007-08	14.00 (25.77)	8.07 (14.85)	8.65 (15.92)	11.75 (21.63)	11.86 (21.83)	54.34
Growth Rates %	14.07	7.74	13.1	9.05	27.04	13.4

Note: Figures in the parenthesis represent percentages.

Source: Field Survey, 2009

Table 5.20: Composition and Trend of Non-Recurring Cost in Professional Colleges (at Constant Prices)

(In ₹ Lakhs)

Items	*Library*	*Construction*	*Equipment*	*Furniture*	*Other expenditure*	*Total*
1997-98	2.14	3.12	1.58	2.37	0.78	9.99
1998-99	2.65	3.53	1.67	4.06	1.41	13.33
1999-00	1.68	2.15	1.62	2.05	1.58	9.08
2000-01	3.50	2.40	2.12	3.38	1.26	12.65
2001-02	3.28	3.83	2.84	2.05	1.34	13.34
2002-03	3.78	3.36	2.59	3.54	0.54	13.81
2003-04	4.34	2.87	2.16	2.87	2.53	14.78
2004-05	3.66	3.06	2.08	2.11	4.16	15.08
2005-06	2.85	4.06	1.90	4.20	3.37	16.38
2006-07	4.01	3.42	3.93	2.81	6.29	20.46
2007-08	6.49	3.74	4.01	5.45	5.50	25.19
Growth Rates %	8.69	2.66	7.78	3.91	21.08	8.09

Source: Field Survey, 2009.

Table 5.21: Composition and Trend of Non-Recurring Cost in Technical Institutions (at Current Prices)

(In ₹ Lakhs)

Items	*Library*	*Construction*	*Equipment*	*Furniture*	*Other expenditure*	*Total*
1997-98	3.29 (18.92)	2.93 (16.83)	5.67 (32.56)	2.15 (12.37)	3.36 (19.32)	17.41
1998-99	5.15 (21.04)	7.39 (30.15)	4.85 (19.78)	2.81 (11.48)	4.30 (17.55)	24.50
1999-00	3.56 (15.71)	4.48 (19.76)	5.16 (22.76)	3.86 (17.03)	5.61 (24.74)	22.69
2000-01	4.81 (17.99)	6.29 (23.55)	6.63 (24.82)	4.00 (14.98)	4.99 (18.66)	26.72
2001-02	1.91 (22.29)	2.19 (25.63)	1.45 (16.93)	1.80 (21.08)	1.20 (14.07)	8.55
2002-03	2.06 (27.25)	1.61 (21.32)	1.42 (18.85)	1.20 (15.86)	1.26 (16.72)	7.55
2003-04						0
2004-05						0
2005-06						0
2006-07						0
2007-08						0
Growth Rates %	–13.35	–16.48	–25.48	–11.35	–22.34	–18.53

Note: Figures in the parentheses represent percentages.

Source: Field Survey, 2009.

Table 5.22: Composition and Trend of Non-Recurring Expenditure (at Constant Prices)

(In ₹ Lakhs)

Year	Library	Construction	Equipment	Furniture	Other expenditure	Total
1997-98	2.48	2.21	4.27	1.62	2.53	13.11
1998-99	3.66	5.25	3.44	2.00	3.06	17.41
1999-00	2.45	3.09	3.55	2.66	3.86	15.62
2000-01	3.09	4.04	4.26	2.57	3.20	17.16
2001-02	1.18	1.36	0.90	1.12	0.75	5.30
2002-03	1.23	0.97	0.85	0.72	0.76	4.53
2003-04						0.00
2004-05						0.00
2005-06						0.00
2006-07						0.00
2007-08						0.00
Growth Rates %	–17.32	–20.25	–28.83	–15.40	–25.83	–22.21

Source: Field Survey, 2009.

Net Public Cost Per Unit

The difference between per unit public cost and fee receipts per student may be regarded as net public cost per unit. This is because of the fact that, educational institutions collect tuition and other fees from the students, which is their income, and hence needs to be subtracted from the expenditure. In order to analyze the trend of net public cost per unit, fee receipts and public cost per unit are presented in Table 5.23.

As to the trend of net public cost per unit the following facts are observed:

(i) The proportion of fee to total public cost per student had increased marginally from 7.84 per cent in 1997-98 to 8.20 per cent in 2007-08. However, the highest contribution of fee to total cost was 12.17 per cent in 1999-2000.

(ii) In real terms, the amount of fee per student had increased from ₹ 812.35 to ₹ 2234.58 between 1997-98 and 2007-08. Thus, fee receipt shows an increasing trend over the period.

(iii) The net public cost per student in current prices increased

4.26 times, i.e., from ₹ 12681.42 to ₹ 53990.28 during the period 1997-98 to 2007-08.

(iv) However, the net cost in real terms rose only 2.62 times, from ₹ 9549.26 to ₹ 25030.26 during the same period.

Table 5.23: Public Cost and Fee Receipt per Student at Current and Constant Prices (1997-98 to 2007-08)

Year	*Current Prices (in ₹)*				*Constant Prices (in ₹)*		
	Cost	*Fee*	*% of Fee to Cost*	*Net Cost*	*Cost*	*Fee*	*Net Cost*
1997-98	13760.22	1078.80	7.84	12681.42	10361.61	812.35	9549.26
1998-99	17567.34	1644.30	9.36	15923.04	12485.67	1168.66	11317.01
1999-00	21672.94	2637.60	12.17	19035.34	14915.99	1815.28	13100.72
2000-01	29500.45	2581.29	8.75	26919.16	18946.98	1657.86	17289.12
2001-02	40992.73	3672.95	8.96	37319.78	25413.97	2277.09	23136.88
2002-03	48441.46	4660.07	9.62	43781.39	29041.64	2793.81	26247.84
2003-04	43622.65	4898.82	11.23	38723.82	24799.69	2785.00	22014.68
2004-05	45838.29	4835.94	10.55	41002.35	24473.19	2581.92	21891.27
2005-06	43179.95	3437.12	7.96	39742.82	22075.64	1757.22	20318.42
2006-07	57642.57	5216.65	9.05	52425.92	27954.69	2529.90	25424.79
2007-08	58810.26	4819.98	8.20	53990.28	27264.84	2234.58	25030.26

Source: Field Survey, 2009

Our hypothesis of highly subsidized higher education in Mizoram is satisfied by the above empirical finding that, the students' contribution was only 12.17 per cent of the total public cost, at the maximum, during the study period. It may, however, be noted here that, public cost consists of only recurring and non-recurring expenditures and excludes the cost of land, buildings and other existent infrastructures thereby rendering it synonymous to institutional cost in the present case.

Relationship between Unit Cost and Enrolment

An attempt has been made, in this section, to see—(i) whether per unit public cost and enrolment are related, at all, and (ii) if related, in which direction—positive or negative? In order to ascertain the twin purpose, regression of unit cost on enrolment was done using Ordinary Least Square (OLS) method for the data given in Table 5.1, at current prices and in Table 5.2, at constant prices. The linear equation used is:

$$Y = b_0 + b_1X$$

where, Y = Unit Cost of Higher Education; and X = Enrolment. In the regression equation 'b_0' is Y intercept and 'b_1' is regression coefficient which shows the rate of change in the cost per student for a unit change in enrolment. The strength of the relationship between the dependent variable Y and the independent variable X has been measured by the coefficient of determination (R^2).

The results of the estimated regression equation are furnished in Table 5.24 and Table 5.25, at current and constant prices, respectively.

Table 5.24: Estimated Regression Equation of Unit Cost on Enrolment (Current Prices)

Sl. No.	*Colleges/Institutions*	*Intercept (b_0)*	*Slope (b_1)*	*R^2*
1.	General Degree Colleges	107734 (30825.57)	–12.89 (5.72)	.36
2.	Professional Colleges	68562.75 (16828.77)	–83.74 (36.5)	.37
3.	Technical Institutions	77482.9 (8111.9)	–73.97 (21.66)	.56
4.	Mizoram University	93624.54 (36340.66)	–9.02* (5.88)	.21

*Insignificant at 5% level of significance.

Note: Figures in the parentheses indicate the standard error of the estimate.
Source: Field Survey, 2009.

It is evident from the negative slope or the negative values of the correlation coefficients both at current and constant prices that an increase in enrolment leads to a fall in unit cost. This is a clear empirical evidence to support the hypothesis about the inverse relationship between enrolment size and per unit public cost of higher education in Mizoram.

Table 5.25: Estimated Regression Equation of Unit Cost on Enrolment (Constant Prices)

Sl. No.	*Colleges/Institutions*	*Intercept (b_0)*	*Slope (b_1)*	*R^2*
1.	General Degree Colleges	60486.44 (10514.4)	–7.23 (1.9)	.60
2.	Professional Colleges	36707.85 (5719.63)	–42.66 (12.41)	.57
3.	Technical Institutions	58498.94 (3660.31)	–77.63 (9.77)	.88
4.	Mizoram University	55747.02 (12717.6)	–5.56 (2.06)	.45

Note: Figures in the parentheses indicate the standard error of the estimate.

Source: Field Survey, 2009.

In terms of current prices, the value of regression coefficient is 9.02 for Mizoram which means that, on an average, a one unit increase in enrolment leads to a fall in public cost by nearly ₹ 9 per student. The value of coefficient of determination (R^2) is 0.21, meaning that approximately 21 per cent of the variation in the unit cost is explained by enrolment levels. In case of General Degree Colleges, the regression coefficient is 12.89, implying a reduction in unit cost by approximately ₹ 13 due to a one unit increase in enrolment. As to the variation in unit cost, 36 per cent is explained by the levels of enrolment as the value of (R^2) is 0.36. The regression coefficient being 83.74 in case of Professional Colleges means a one unit increase in enrolment results in fall in unit cost by approximately ₹ 84. The coefficient of determination (R^2) with its value of 0.37 implies that almost 37 per cent of the variation in unit cost is determined by enrolment. Finally, the value of regression coefficient in case of Technical Institutions is 73.97, which means that a one unit increase in enrolment reduces unit cost by nearly ₹ 74. With the value of (R^2) being 0.56, almost 56 per cent of the variation in unit cost is explained by enrolment levels.

However, in real terms, a one unit increase in enrolment results into a fall in unit cost by nearly ` 6 in case of Mizoram and ` 7, ` 43, and ` 78 in case of General Degree Colleges, Professional Colleges and Technical Institutions, respectively. As to the variation in unit cost, 60 per cent is explained by enrolment in case of General Degree

Colleges, 57 per cent in case of Professional Colleges, 88 per cent in case of Technical Institutions and 45 per cent in case of Mizoram, as a whole.

Optimum Enrolment Size and Unit Cost

Optimum enrolment means the size of enrolment that minimizes cost per unit. In the present exercise second degree polynomial function is used to estimate the optimum enrolment size. The quadratic equation used is:

$$Y = b_0 + b_1X + b_2X^2$$

where, Y = Unit Cost of Higher Education; and X = Enrolment.

The optimum enrolment was determined by following the simple optimization techniques of calculus as follows:

First Order Condition: $dy/dx = 0$
Second order Condition: $d^2y/dx^2 > 0$; Minimum
< 0; Maximum

The results of the estimated functions are presented in Table 5.26.

Table 5.26: Quadratic Cost Function of Different Institutions

Sl. No.	*Colleges/ Institutions*	b_0	b_1	b_2	R^2	*Optimum Enrolment*
1.	General Degree Colleges	–31827.63*	27.51*	–0.0032*	.66	4298.44**
2.	Professional Colleges	9464.83*	77.93*	–0.13*	.61	599.6**
3.	Technical Institutions	79543.31	–246.36	0.26	.94	947.54
4.	Mizoram	–47856.27*	28.51*	–0.003*	.51	9503.33**

* Insignificant at 5% level of significance.

** Since the level of enrolment that minimizes unit cost cannot be estimated, the level of enrolment that maximizes cost is given.

Note: With the exception of technical institutions the estimated parameters are found to be insignificant at 5 per cent level. This is technically due to the presence of multicollinearity in the regression. It is also, on *a priori* ground, believed that X and X^2 are highly correlated. This is the main cause of multicollinearity in the present exercise. Though the estimates are insignificant, the estimated variation or coefficient of determination (R^2) is quite high for all colleges. So, it is believed that calculation of optimum level of enrolment could still be reasonable. Further, application of functional types other than quadratic function (like cubic, semi-log, etc.) would increase the problem of multicollinearity in the estimation.

Source: Field Survey, 2009.

The above table reveals that, the estimation of optimum enrolment size resulted into both minimum and maximum number of students for different types of higher educational institutions. The optimum level of enrolment that minimizes unit cost in Technical Institutions was calculated to be 948 students. As for the whole state of Mizoram as well as for the General Degree Colleges and for the Professional Colleges the level of enrolment that minimizes unit cost could not be estimated. However, the levels of enrolment that maximizes unit cost in Mizoram and the two types of colleges are found to be 9503, 4298 and 600 number of students, respectively. Any deviation from these numbers will lead to a reduction in the per unit public cost.

Private Cost of Higher Education

Students and their families spend substantial amounts of money to acquire education in different courses and levels of studies which may broadly be termed as private cost of education. Assessment of private cost of education furnishes information relating to the extent of burden borne by households of different income and occupational groups as well as the amount of cost covered by subsidy in the form of grants and scholarships.

The analysis of direct private costs of education along with the estimates of opportunity costs can furnish solution to some of the issues and problems encountered in underdeveloped countries such as, the early dropout rate of poor families and irregular attendance of children belonging to agricultural families during busy seasons (Blaug, 1966). The information on private cost is absolutely essential to make proper planning of resources for education in general, and to plan for public expenditure on scholarships, stipends, etc., in particular. Ignoring these aspects is too costly, resulting in a wide gap between the expected (or planned) enrolments and actual enrolments (Tilak and Verghese, 1983).

Since the adoption of the 'structural adjustment' of the IMF (in India since 1991) and the economic reforms of the 1990s, social sector expenditures were reduced and education has been the main casualty. This gave rise to an intensive discussion about the need for enhancing fees charged by educational institutions and reducing the elements of subsidy at the higher levels of education. The information with regard to the components of private cost of higher education is, therefore, essential for educational planners and policy-makers to assess the magnitude of private investment in education and to determine the extent to which households will be able to meet the direct and indirect cost of education.

In the following section an attempt has been made to analyze the private cost of higher education in Mizoram. The discussion mainly centred around the various components of private cost and the socio-economic background of the students.

Components of Private Cost

Total private cost has been decomposed into: (i) fee (admission, tuition and other non-refundable fees), (ii) books, stationery, internet, etc., (iii) accommodation (room rent/hostel fee), (iv) food (including tiffin), (v) conveyance, and (vi) personal maintenance (clothing, health care, sports etc.).

Table 5.27 reveals that, on an average, a student pays an amount of ₹ 5801.32 as fee with a standard deviation of ₹ 7546.07 per annum. The minimum amount of fee was ₹ 3190 and the maximum amount was ₹ 62500 per year. The average cost of books and stationeries were calculated at ₹ 5103.18, while the standard deviation was ₹ 1463.74 per annum. The expenditure on this item varied between ₹ 2500 and ₹ 13000 per year. The average cost of accommodation incurred by a student was ₹ 11430.43 per annum, and the standard deviation was ₹ 3175.77 among different students. The minimum expenditure incurred on accommodation by a student was ₹ 200 and the maximum amount was ₹ 16000 per annum. On food items the

Table 5.27: Components of Private Cost in Mizoram, 2007-08

Components	*Mean (₹)*	*Standard Deviation (₹)*	*Minimum (₹)*	*Maximum (₹)*	*Coefficient of Variation (CV)*
Fee	5801.32	7546.07	3190	62500	1.3008
Books, etc.	5103.18	1463.74	2500	13000	0.2868
Accommodation	11430.43	3175.77	200	16000	0.2778
Food	14757.73	1365.12	7000	17400	0.0925
Conveyance	3060.73	1266.17	400	7600	0.4137
Personal maint.	4940.91	1079.56	3500	10200	0.2185
Total (Average)	40819.95	11118.75	24200	110300	0.2724

Source: Field Survey, 2009

average expenditure of a student was estimated at ₹ 14757.73, with a deviation of ₹ 1365.12 per year. The range of minimum and maximum expenditure on food was ₹ 7000 and ₹ 17400, respectively. The students spend, on an average, ₹ 3060.73 on annual conveyance, and the deviation calculated among different students was ₹ 1266.17. The expenditure on this item varied between the minimum of ₹ 400 to the maximum of ₹ 7600 per year. The average expenditure on personal maintenance was estimated at ₹ 4940.91, with a standard deviation of ₹ 1079.56 per annum. The minimum expenditure incurred on this item was ₹ 3500 and the maximum amount was ₹ 10200 per year.

The total private cost, on an average, was estimated at ₹ 40819.95 with the standard deviation of ₹ 11118.75 per annum. The minimum and maximum amount spent annually was ₹ 24200 and ₹ 110300, respectively.

The variability of the data series or the consistency of the data has been measured by the Coefficient of Variation (CV). From the above Table it is seen that, the components of private cost varied between 9 per cent and 130 per cent. The value of coefficient of variation was the lowest at 9 per cent in case of the expenditure on food items, while the degree of variation was the highest at 130 per cent in case of fees. The second highest value of coefficient of variation was estimated at 41 per cent in case of conveyance expenses. The degree of variation in the expenditure on books and stationeries was found to be 29 per cent and the same had slightly declined to

28 per cent for the cost of accommodation, and had finally reached 22 per cent in case of the expenditure on personal maintenance. However, the value of coefficient of variation was estimated at 27 per cent for the total private cost of higher education in Mizoram.

In Table 5.28 the average private cost of education under different types of institutions is presented. The table shows that the average fee per student was the highest in ICFAI University. It was ₹ 26625.00 per student in 2007-08. Wide variation is seen in the expenditure on this item. Cost of fee per student in General Degree Colleges was ₹ 3735.94 per annum, which is the lowest. Average fee per student was estimated at ₹ 5049.00, ₹ 5675.00 and ₹ 7070.56 in Professional Colleges, Technical Institutions and Mizoram University, respectively.

The average expenditure on books and stationeries was the highest at ₹ 6450.00 in Professional Colleges and the lowest at ₹ 4612.50 in Technical Institutions. It was ₹ 5547.22 in Mizoram University and ₹ 4981.88 in General Degree Colleges. The per capita expenditure on this item in ICFAI University was ₹ 5025.00 per annum.

Table 5.28: Components of Private Cost Under Different Institutions, 2007-08

(Amount in ₹)

Institution	*Fee*	*Books etc.*	*Accomo-dation.*	*Food*	*Conveyance*	*Personal mainten-ance*
Degree Colleges	3735.94	4981.88	11195.20	15060.10	2735.04	4973.91
Professional Colleges	5049.00	6450.00	13157.10	13370.00	4430.00	5430.00
Technical Institutions	5675.00	4612.50	8481.25	12116.70	3304.17	5208.33
Mizoram University	7070.56	5547.22	12966.70	15502.80	3338.89	4394.44
ICFAI University	26625.00	5025.00	13650.00	15483.30	4316.67	5258.33
Total (Average)	5801.32	5103.18	11430.40	14757.70	3060.73	4940.91

Source: Field Survey, 2009.

Per student expenditure on accommodation was the highest in ICFAI University. It was ₹ 13650.00 per year. In Technical Institutions it was quite low at ₹ 8481.25, as there are adequate hostel facilities and students are not required to pay high rent in private houses. In General Degree Colleges, Professional Colleges and Mizoram University per student expenditure on accommodation were ₹ 11195.20, ₹ 13157.10 and ₹ 12966.70, respectively.

The mean expenditure on food was ₹ 12116.70 in Technical Institutions and ₹ 13370.00 in Professional Colleges per student per year. In case of General Degree Colleges, Mizoram University and ICFAI University the average spending on food figured at ₹ 15060.10, ₹ 15502.80 and ₹ 15483.30, respectively.

As regards conveyance, per capita spending varied between a low of ₹ 2735.04 in General Degree Colleges and a high of ₹ 4430.00 in Professional Colleges. It was ₹ 4316.67 in ICFAI University, ₹ 3338.89 in Mizoram University and ₹ 3304.17 in Technical Institutions per annum.

On an average, a student of Professional College spends ₹ 5430.00 on personal maintenance in a year. ICFAI University students spend the second highest amount of ₹ 5258.33 per capita. Average expenditure on the same item was ₹ 5208.33, ₹ 4973.91 and ₹ 4394.44 in Technical Institutions, General Degree Colleges and Mizoram University, respectively.

Table 5.29 represents the breakup of private cost in different courses of higher study in Mizoram. It is seen that the average fee of ICFAI University courses are the highest, where MBA with an annual fee of ₹ 62500.00 tops the list. On the contrary, the lowest amount of fee estimated was ₹ 3602.74 per annum for B.A. course.

Average fee were also low at ₹ 3902.78 and ₹ 3963.33 for B.Com and B.Sc. courses, respectively. Per capita fee for LLB and Technical courses were bit higher at ₹ 5049.00 and ₹ 5675.00, respectively. The same was estimated at ₹ 12000.00 for both BBA and BHTM, while ₹ 20000.00 was the fee for BCA course. For BE course, the average fee paid by a student was ₹ 24000.00. Average fee for post graduate courses again is low at ₹ 4780.00 for M.Com., ₹ 4930.00 for MA and ₹ 5050.00 for M.Sc. per annum.

Per student expenditure on books for BE course was the highest at ₹ 10125.00 and the lowest at ₹ 4000.00 for BBA per year. For all

Table 5.29: Components of Private Cost in Different Courses of Higher Education, 2007-08

(Amount in ₹)

Course	Fee	Books etc.	Accomo-dation	Food	Convey-ance	Personal maintenace
B.A.	3602.74	4473.81	11277.60	15072.60	2659.64	4883.33
B.Com.	3902.78	5416.67	11346.20	14861.10	3616.67	5522.22
B.Sc.	3963.33	5950.00	10909.50	15130.60	2468.06	4911.11
LLB	5049.00	6450.00	13157.10	13370.00	4430.00	5430.00
Technical	5675.00	4612.50	8481.25	12116.70	3304.17	5208.33
BBA	12000.00	4000.00	12900.00	15600.00	4000.00	5166.67
BCA	20000.00	5000.00	14500.00	15666.70	4333.33	5000.00
BHTM	12000.00	5000.00	13200.00	15300.00	3933.33	5500.00
M.A.	4930.00	4058.33	12225.00	15141.70	3308.33	4550.00
M.Com.	4780.00	4266.67	12400.00	15833.30	3100.00	4133.33
M.Sc.	5050.00	6064.29	13733.30	15571.40	3357.14	4414.29
BE (MZU)	24000.00	10125.00	13900.00	15850.00	3725.00	4250.00
MBA(ICFAI)	62500.00	6100.00	14000.00	15366.70	5000.00	5366.67
Total (Average)	5801.32	5103.18	11430.40	14757.70	3060.73	4940.91

Source: Field Survey, 2009

other courses average spending on books etc., ranged between ₹ 4058.33 (MA) and ₹ 6100.00 (MBA). The amount of expenditure on this item did not vary much among the rest of the courses.

Students of Technical courses spend ₹ 8481.25 per capita on accommodation, which is the least. As for the students of other courses, per capita expenditure on this item averaged between the low of ₹ 10909.50 (in B.Sc.) and the high of ₹ 14500.00 (in BCA) per year.

The mean expenditure on food mostly hovered around ₹ 15072.60 to ₹ 15850.00 for the students of BA and BE courses, respectively. The exceptions were observed in per student's spending on food of Technical, professional (LLB) and B.Com. courses at ₹ 12116.70, ₹ 13370.00 and ₹ 14861.10, respectively.

The lowest amount spent on annual conveyance was calculated at ₹ 2468.06 and the highest amount at ₹ 5000.00 per student of B.Sc. and MBA course, respectively. The second lowest expenditure on annual conveyance was ₹ 2659.64 for BA students. On an average, an LLB student spent ₹ 4430.00, a BCA student spent ₹ 4333.33 and a BBA student spent ₹ 4000.00 per annum on this item. It ranged from ₹ 3100.00 to ₹ 3933.33 per capita for the students of rest of the courses.

The highest amount of expenditure on personal maintenance per student was estimated at ₹ 5522.22 for B.Com. course followed by ₹ 5500.00 for BHTM, ₹ 5430 for LLB, ₹ 5366.67 for MBA, ₹ 5208.33 for Technical courses, ₹ 5166.67 for BBA and ₹ 5000.00 for BCA course. The least expenditure on this item at ₹ 4133.33 per capita per year was incurred by M.Com. students. It was marginally higher at ₹ 4250.00 for the students of BE, at ₹ 4414.29 for M.Sc. and at ₹ 4550.00 for MA students. While a B.Sc. student spent, on an average, ₹ 4911.11 annually on personal maintenance, it slightly declined to ₹ 4883.33 for the students pursuing BA course.

Private Cost and Socio-Economic Background

In this section an attempt is made to analyze the direct private cost of higher education borne by the students and their parents *vis-à-vis* their socio-economic status. Private cost is greatly influenced by the socio-economic condition of a student, and socio-economic condition, in turn, depends on the income of the household and occupational background of parents. Because of the above fact, the students are divided according to parental occupation in Table 5.30. It is seen from the table that, government servants happen to be the biggest occupational group of parents claiming 53.18 per cent of the students, while only 8.64 per cent students are hailed from the families with agriculture and allied activities as their occupation. Business class sends 21.36 per cent students to higher education and the rest 16.82 per cent pupils are the children of the self-employed people.

Table 5.30 also reveals that, the occupational group of government servants not only claims more than half of the student population but also comprises the largest number of pupils from all the courses, except for BE in which business group records the highest and for BHTM where self-employed class ranks the highest.

Agriculture and the allied sector, on the other hand, represents the least number of students from each course, except from B.Sc. and BE where its position is better than that of the self-employed class.

Table 5.30: Parental Occupation and Course-wise Number of Students in 2007-08

Course	Agri. & Allied	Business	Govt. Service	Self-Employed	Total
B.A.	8	13	47	16	84
B.Com.	1	4	9	4	18
B.Sc.	4	10	19	3	36
LLB		1	8	1	10
Technical	2	7	9	6	24
BBA		1	2		3
BCA			2	1	3
BHTM			1	2	3
M.A.	1	3	7	1	12
M.Com.	1	2	2	1	6
M.Sc.	1	3	8	2	14
BE (MZU)	1	2	1		4
MBA (ICFAI)		1	2		3
Total	19	47	117	37	220

Source: Field Survey, 2009.

The occupational category of self-employed parents occupies the second highest position in the number of B.A. students and has an edge over the agricultural families in respect of students in B.A., B.Com., M.Sc. and Technical courses. Self-employed category is at least equal in rank to agricultural one in respect of M.A. and M.Com., and also to business group of parents with regard to LLB course.

The relative position of business class in terms of students is seen to be second in M.Sc., M.A., B.Sc. and Technical courses, third in B.A. course and at least equal to the rank of government service category in M.Com. course.

Parental income of the students has been approximated into seven groups to examine the influence of income on enrolment. The income groups are: (a) ₹ 0 to ₹ 100000; (b) ₹ 100000 to ₹ 150000; (c) ₹ 150000 to ₹ 200000; (d) ₹ 200000 to ₹ 250000; (e) ₹ 250000 to ₹ 300000; (f) ₹ 300000 to ₹ 350000; and (g) ₹ 350000 and above. The distribution of students according to their annual family income and parental occupation is given in Table 5.31.

Table 5.31 shows that, out of the total number of students 23.64 per cent belonged to ₹ 100000 to ₹ 150000 income group and 23.18 per cent belong to the income group of ₹ 150000 to ₹ 200000. Thus the above two income groups together accounts for 46.82 per cent of

Table 5.31 : Number of Students with Parental Occupation and Family Income, 2007-08

Income In (₹)	*Agri. & allied*	*Business*	*Govt. Service*	*Self-employed*	*Total*
	Parents Occupation				
0-100000	11	3	2	8	24
100000-150000	7	5	34	6	52
150000-200000		14	28	9	51
200000-250000	1	15	23	6	45
250000-300000		6	17	3	26
300000-350000		3	10	2	15
350000 - and above		1	3	3	7

Source: Field Survey, 2009.

students in higher education. Another important income group is ₹ 200000 to ₹ 250000 which accounts for 20.45 per cent of the total enrolment. Only 11.82 per cent and 10.91 per cent students come from ₹ 250000 to ₹ 300000 and ₹ 0 to ₹ 100000 income group, respectively. Another 6.82 per cent students belonged to ₹ 300000 to ₹ 350000 income group. The least number of students, constituting only 3.18 per cent, are hailed from the group with income of ₹ 350000 and above.

As to the distribution of students according to the occupational background of their parents, Table 5.31 shows that, the largest number, i.e. 14.45 per cent of the students are from the category of government servants with an annual income of ₹ 100000 to ₹ 150000. On the other hand, the lowest number, i.e. only 0.45 per cent of the students belonged to the agricultural families with an income of ₹ 200000 to ₹ 250000 per year. Similarly, the businessmen of the income group of ₹ 350000 and above send 0.45 per cent of the students to the higher educational institutions in Mizoram.

Table 5.32 presents the number of students according to their course of study and family income. It is seen that, from the families with income range of ₹ 0 to ₹ 100000 per annum 41.67 per cent students were studying BA, 25 per cent studying B.Com., 16.67 per cent studying B.Sc. and 4.17 per cent studying each of the M.A., M.Sc., BE and Technical courses in 2007-08. In the second income group of ₹ 100000 to ₹ 150000 the number of students pursuing different courses was: 44.23 per cent from B.A., 19.23 per cent from B.Sc., 7.69 per cent from each of M.A. and M.Sc., 5.77 per cent from each of M.Com. and Technical courses, 3.85 per cent from each of BE and B.Com., and 1.92 per cent from LLB. The income group ₹ 150000 to ₹ 200000 represented 23.18 per cent of the total number of students, out of which 39.22 per cent belonged to B.A., at the maximum, and 1.96 per cent belonged to each of the BCA, BHTM and M.Com. course, at the minimum. In the income group ₹ 200000 to ₹ 250000, 40 per cent students went for B.A., 17.78 per cent for Technical courses, 6.67 per cent for each of the B.Sc., M.A. and M.Sc. course, 4.44 per cent each for BBA, BCA and M.Com., and 2.22 per cent for each of B.Com, LLB, BHTM and MBA courses. Out of the total number of students only 11.82 per cent belonged to the income group of ₹ 250000 to ₹ 300000. This group accounted for 34.62 per cent pupils in B.A., 11.54 per cent each in B.Sc., M.Sc. and Technical courses, 7.69 per cent each in B.Com., LLB and MBA, and 3.85 per cent each in BBA and M.A. courses. The families with an annual income of ₹ 300000 to ₹ 350000 bagged 6.82 per cent of the total student strength, of which 33.33 per cent went for B.Sc.,

Table 5.32 : Course-wise Number of Students with Family Income, 2007-08

	Family Income (in ₹)							
Course	*0–100000*	*100000 to 150000*	*150000 to 200000*	*200000 to 250000*	*250000 to 300000*	*300000 to 350000*	*350000 and above*	*Total*
B.A.	10	23	20	18	9	4		84
B.Com.	6	2	5	1	2	1	1	18
B.Sc.	4	10	9	3	3	5	2	36
LLB		1	5	1	2	1		10
Technical	1	3	5	8	3	1	3	24
BBA				2	1			3
BCA			1	2				3
BHTM			1	1			1	3
M.A.	1	4	2	3	1	1		12
M.Com.		3	1	2				6
M.Sc.	1	4	2	3	3	1		14
BE (MZU)	1	2				1		4
MBA (ICFAI)				1	2			3
Total	**24**	**52**	**51**	**45**	**26**	**15**	**7**	**220**

Source: Field Survey, 2009.

26.67 per cent went for B.A. and 6.67 per cent went for each of the B.Com., LLB, M.A., M.Sc., BE and Technical courses. The highest income group of ₹ 350000 and above accounted for only 3.18 per cent of the total number of students. The course-wise distribution of students of this group shows that 42.86 per cent students studied Technical courses, 28.57 per cent studied B.Sc., and 14.29 per cent studied each of the B.Com. and BHTM course in 2007-08.

Table 5.33 shows the mean expenditure of families with different levels of income on all the items of private cost. On an average, the highest amount of expenditure on all the items of private cost calculated at ₹ 47457 was incurred by the families with an annual income of ₹ 350000 and above in 2007-08. The second highest amount at ₹ 44946 were spent by ₹ 250000 to ₹ 300000 income group families. This was followed by ₹ 42961 and ₹ 42446 incurred by the income group of ₹ 300000 to ₹ 350000 and ₹ 200000 to ₹ 250000, respectively. The next three groups spent comparatively lower amount. It was ₹ 39371 by the income group of ₹ 100000 to ₹ 150000, ₹ 39289 by the group earning between ₹ 150000 and ₹ 200000 and finally ₹ 36419 by the families that earn up to ₹ 100000 per annum.

Table 5.33: Components of Private Cost Under Different Income Groups in 2007-08

(Amount in ₹)

Components	*Income groups*						
	0–100000	*100000–150000*	*150000–200000*	*200000–250000*	*250000–300000*	*300000–350000*	*350000 and above*
Fee	4804	4797	4717	6886	9056	5501	6157
Books, etc.	5106	4938	5225	4931	5154	5407	5700
Accomodation	10889	11813	11231	10718	11639	12042	13300
Food	14725	15000	14643	14793	14469	14873	14500
Conveyance	2388	2887	3101	3295	3367	2993	3900
Personal maint.	5313	4708	5216	4753	4842	4553	5800
Total (Average)	36419	39371	39289	42446	44946	42961	47457

Source: Field Survey, 2009.

It is also evident from this table that, the mean expenditure on food claimed the highest amount of expenditure across all income groups.

This was followed by the average expenditure on accommodation. Expenditure on food records the highest at ₹ 15000 incurred by the students' families with an annual income ranging between ₹ 100000 to ₹ 150000, while the lowest amount spent on this item was ₹ 14469 by the families in the income group of ₹ 250000 to ₹ 300000. Regarding the rest of the items, except on fee the highest income group of families, viz. ₹ 350000 and above spent the largest amount of ₹ 5800 on personal maintenance, ₹ 3900 on conveyance, ₹ 13300 on accommodation and ₹ 5700 on books and stationeries. The minimum expenditure on these items were ₹ 4553 by the income group of ₹ 300000 to ₹ 350000, ₹ 2388 by the income group of ₹ 0 to ₹ 100000, ₹ 10718 by the income group of ₹ 200000 to ₹ 250000 and ₹ 4931 by the same income group, respectively. However, the average amount of fee at ₹ 9056 paid by the families of ₹ 250000 to ₹ 300000 income group was seen to be the maximum and at ₹ 4717 incurred by the families earning between ₹ 150000 to ₹ 200000 per year as the minimum.

Net Private Cost per Unit

During the course of study, generally, students receive some amount of money from the government by way of subsidies, particularly in the form of book grants, tribal scholarships, etc. These are income received but not earned or 'transfer payments' which need to be deducted from the private cost in order to arrive at the net private cost. Net private cost is the cost which is actually borne by the students and their parents.

In the estimation of per unit private cost it was found that all students received a scholarship and the average of which is provided in Table 5.34. The average scholarship received by a student in the

Table 5.34: Net Private Cost of Higher Education in Mizoram, 2007-08

Private Cost (in ₹)	*Scholarship (in ₹)*	*Percentage of Scholarship to Cost*	*Net Private Cost (in ₹) (1-2)*
1	2	4	5
40819.95	3306.69	8.10	37513.26

Source: Field Survey, 2009

higher educational institutions in Mizoram was calculated at ₹ 3306.69 in the year 2007-08. The table also reveals that, on an average the private cost per unit was ₹ 40819.95 in the same year. Thus, the net private cost per student worked out to be ₹ 37513.26 in Mizoram.

The percentage contribution of scholarship to cost is only 8.10 per cent. This means that the major share, i.e., 91.90 per cent of private cost is contributed by the households in Mizoram.

Total Cost of Higher Education in Mizoram

In this section an attempt has been made to estimate the total cost of higher education in Mizoram. Total cost of education incorporates public cost, private cost and opportunity cost. As opportunity cost has been kept outside the purview of this study, the total cost of higher education is estimated by adding up the net public cost and net private cost. This is shown in Table 5.35

Table 5.35: Average Total Cost of Higher Education in Mizoram, 2007-08

Sl. No.	*Particulars*	*Amount (in ₹)*
1.	Public Cost	58810.26
2.	Fee	4819.98
3.	Net Public Cost	53990.28
4.	Private Cost	40819.95
5.	Scholarship	3306.69
6.	Net Private Cost	37513.26
7.	Total Cost of Higher Education (3+6)	91503.54

Source: Field Survey, 2009.

Net public cost and net private cost per unit were arrived at by deducting the transfer payments, viz. average fee from the former and scholarship per student from the latter.

The total cost of higher education was estimated at ₹ 91503.54 per student in 2007-08. It is the sum total of net public cost at ₹ 53990.28 and net private cost at ₹ 37513.54 per student per annum. It is observed that the net public cost is 1.44 times higher than the net private cost. This, in fact, validates our hypothesis that public cost per unit is greater than per unit private cost of higher education. Thus, it is found that the public authorities shoulder greater burden than do the students and their families in financing higher education in Mizoram.

REFERENCES

Blaug, M. (1970), *An Introduction into the Economics of Education*, Penguin, London.

Tilak, J.B.G. and V.N. Verghese (1983), *Resources for Education in India* Occasional Paper, No. 2, NIEPA, New Delhi.

6

Sources of Finance for Higher Education

Introduction

It is now well recognized that the growth of the global economy has increased opportunities for those countries with good levels of education and *vice versa* (Carnoy, 1999; Tilak, 2001; Stewart, 1996; Ilon, 1994). The benefits of globalization accrue to the countries with highly skilled human capital and it is a curse for the countries without such specialized human capital. Developing countries are further challenged in a highly competitive world economy because their higher education systems are not adequately developed for the creation and use of knowledge. Converting the challenges into opportunities depend on the quantum and system of finance for their education sector. Though the higher education system and the pattern of financing higher education vary a great deal across countries in terms of their size and strength and degree of diversification of higher education institutions, yet they all face a severe financial crisis in the public finances available for higher education.

In India too, the economic reform packages, introduced under the New Economic Policy since 1991, imposed a heavy compression on the public budgets on education sector, more specifically so on higher education. The shares of non-governmental sources such as fees and voluntary contributions have also been declining. At the same time the needs of the higher education system have been growing rapidly. It is being increasingly realized that public budgets cannot adequately fund higher education, particularly when sectors of mass education are starved of even bare needs. Hence, of late several policy proposals are made, including 'privatization'. Consequently, the need for experimentation with several alternatives, including student fees, students loans, graduate tax, and privatization in general is emphasized.

In the present chapter an attempt has been made to examine the various sources of finance for education, in general, and higher education, in particular. The last part of the chapter deals with the sources of fund for higher education in Mizoram with their relative importance.

Sources of Finance for Education

The sources of finance for education in developing countries like India may broadly be classified into: (1) external sources, and (2) internal sources.

The external sources of finance can further be divided into the following three categories:

(a) *International Institutions* – of which the World Bank is the most important, as it provides finance for various types of educational projects, particularly for lower levels of education.
(b) *Foreign Governments* – which are particularly important for financing specialized courses in higher education, viz. language courses and literature based on these languages. It also includes various types of scholarships offered by foreign governments to scholars in India.
(c) *International Private Agencies (NGOs)* – of which Ford Foundation, Rockfeller Foundation, etc., are very important. These private trusts provide various types of liberal educational grants.

The internal sources of finance may broadly be categorized into:

(a) Private sources, and
(b) Public or government sources.

Private sources of finance for education can again be: (i) compulsory, and (ii) voluntary in nature. Compulsory private sources include students' fees and other related charges. Voluntary private sources include endowments, trust funds, donations, grants, gifts and other types of voluntary financial help. Some educational institutions also raise funds from sale of publications and income from institutional assets.

Public or government sources consist of funds received from: (i) central or federal government, (ii) state governments, and (iii) local bodies.

Thus, the different sources of finance for education may be summarized in terms of the following figure:

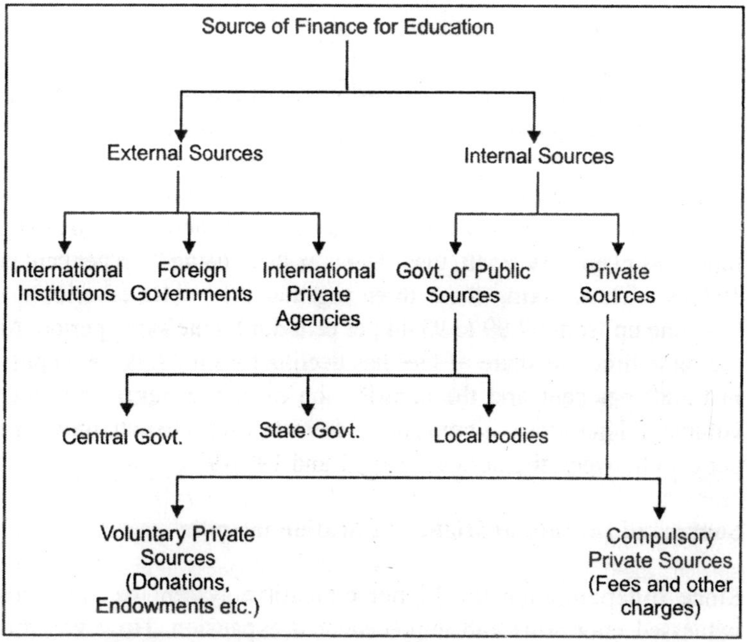

Sources of Finance for Education in India

The main sources of finance for the education sector in India comprise government funds, local body funds, university funds, fees, endowments and others. The available data on these sources are presented in Table 6.1.

Table 6.1: Sources of Income for all Educational Institutions in India

(*Percentage*)

Year	Govt. funds (Centre & States)	Local body funds	University funds	Total Public Funds	Fees	Endowments and other sources	Total
1	2	3	4	5	6	7	8
1950-51	57.06	10.39	—	67.99	20.39	11.62	100
1960-61	67.97	6.53	—	74.50	17.14	8.35	100
1970-71	75.65	4.34	1.36	81.35	12.81	5.85	100
1980-81	81.70	4.71	1.37	87.78	8.20	4.03	100
1985-86	80.29	5.23	2.15	87.67	6.27	6.06	100
1990-91	87.87	6.22	0.01	94.10	3.53	2.37	100
1991-92	86.35	7.08	0.01	93.44	3.82	2.74	100

Source: Economic Survey, 1998-99.

Table 6.1 shows that the contribution of government funds has gone up from 57.06 per cent in 1950-51 to 86.35 per cent in 1991-92. It includes contribution of both Central and State Governments. The contribution of local body funds has come down from 10.93 per cent in 1950-51 to 7.08 per cent in 1991-92. The contribution of university funds has been very small, the maximum share being 2.15 per cent in 1985-86. Thus, taking these three together the public contribution has gone up from 67.99 to 93.44 per cent during the same period. At the same time the share of fees has declined from 20.39 per cent to just 3.82 per cent and the contribution of endowments and other voluntary donations has come down from 11.62 per cent to only 2.74 per cent between the period 1950-51 and 1991-92.

Sources of Income of Higher Education in India

Since Independence the higher education system in India has witnessed enormous and unprecedented expansion. However, this expansion is not accompanied by commensurate financial allocations by government, both at the central level as well as at the state level. Nor have universities and colleges been able to raise adequate finances of their own. New universities have been started without providing additional resources and the universities on their part have not generated much resources of their own. There has been, as a result, an exclusive dependence on the government for financing higher education. The government, on its part, is finding it difficult to shoulder the heavy responsibility of financing higher education on account of competing demands from other sectors of an expanding economy.

Higher education in India receives funds mainly from public and private sources. Public sources include the Central Government, State Governments, the University Grants Commission, government agencies like Indian Council for Agricultural Research, Council for Scientific and Industrial Research, etc., for specific projects. Private sources include fees, endowments and donations, internal sources of income like the press, university publications, income from movable and immovable property, sale of farm produce, etc. Though a significant contribution can be made from these sources, the universities have not displayed enough dynamism in exploiting these sources to their advantage. As for endowments and donations, their importance as a significant source of income has dried up. This may be on account of inflationary trends, a change in the attitudes of the public towards charity, less significant tax advantages and so on.

Public financing has thus increased both in absolute and relative terms. There is also a strong justification of public financing of higher education. Higher education has generally been recognized as a "public good", at least as a "quasi-public good" (CABE, 2005). The public good nature of higher education warrants that the state should play a more active role in the financing of higher education. Thus, allocative efficiency as well as distributional considerations also justifies public funding of higher education.

The sources of financing higher education can broadly be classified into:

1. Fees,
2. Government,
3. Endowments and others.

Table 6.2 shows the relative significance of these three sources. The available data in the table reveals that, the contribution of government source has increased, while the shares of fees and endowments have declined considerably, during the period 1950-51 to 1994-95. The percentage contribution of government in financing higher education increased from 57 in 1950-51 to 83 in 1994-95. As for the contribution of fees it fell down from 20 to 9 per cent during 1950-51 to 1994-95. Similarly, the share of endowments and others declined from 23 per cent to only 8 per cent during the same period.

Table 6.2: Sources of Income of Higher Education in India

(*Percentage*)

Year	*Government*	*Fees*	*Endowments and Others*
1950-51	57	20	23
1960-61	68	17	15
1970-71	76	13	11
1980-81	82	8	10
1983-84	82	8	10
1991-92	83	8	9
1994-95	83	9	8

Source: 1. G.R. Reddy: "Financing of Higher Education in India" in *Perspectives in Education* 1995, Vol. II (No.1). 2. *Educational Expenditure in India*, MHRD, Government of India, New Delhi, 1995.

It is evident from the above analysis that governmental source is the prime source of finance for higher education. In fact, such a rapid growth in public financing of higher education in India has been necessary for the following reasons:

- Facilities for higher education available at the time of independence were insignificant. Independence had created an abnormal increase in the social demand for higher education, and public expenditure has had to cope with the demand.
- Building up a new socio-economic system after the end of the colonial rule required large scale manpower with varied skills; so the government had to expand investment in higher education.
- The very development models emphasized high skilled labour force, and building up of huge social infrastructure for excellence in science and technology, and research and development.

- Government policies towards equality in education led to the growth in public investment in education, since it involves huge subsidies at all levels of education to a substantial number of students, belonging to weaker sections.
- The rapid growth of school education naturally pushed the demand for higher education.

The government is seen to spend too much on higher education and many question the wisdom of the government in doing so, especially when other sectors of the economy are starved of funds. However, the fact is that, public expenditure on education in India is much less as compared to the developed as well as many of the developing countries of the world.

Table 6.3 : Public Expenditure on Education Sector and Higher Education as Percentage of GDP in Selected Countries

Country	*Year*	*Total Education*	*Higher Education*
Malaysia	2002	8.1	2.7
Sweden	2002	7.6	2.2
Tunisia	2002	6.4	1.5
USA	2002	5.6	1.4
Australia	2002	5.7	1.3
UK	2002	5.3	1.1
Thailand	2002-03	5.0	1.0
Argentina	2002	4.0	0.7
India	2001-02	3.4	0.7
Chile	2002	4.4	0.6
Russian Federation	2002	3.7	0.6
Philippines	2002	3.1	0.4

Source: UNESCO-UIS/OECD 2005 'Education Trends in Perspective-Analysis of the World Education Indicators'.

As is seen in Table 6.3, the public expenditure on both total education and higher education as percentage of Gross Domestic Product is much lower in India than what we find in many other countries of the world. While in Malaysia 8.1 per cent of GDP was spent on education in 2002, in India it was only 3.4 per cent in 2001-02. Similarly, only 0.7 per cent of GDP was spent on higher education as against 2.7 per cent in Malaysia, 2.2 per cent in Sweden and 1.5 per cent in Tunisia. We can, therefore, conclude that state financing of education in India is quite low when seen in the global context. This is in contradiction to the thrust being given to the social sector development in India in recent years, as education is an important component of the social sector.

An analysis of the government spending on higher and technical education in India is made in Table 6.4. It is revealed that, the public expenditure as percentage of GNP has declined from 0.61 to 0.34 during 1990-91 to 2004-05. Likewise, out of the total budget the share devoted to higher and technical education was 2.09 per cent in 1990-91, which had fallen down to 1.60 per cent in 2004-05. Thus, public fund as percentage of both GNP and total budget shows a declining trend during the one and half decade. Another fact the table reveals is that only a meagre proportion the total budget and GNP is spent on this sector. In other words, much less than 1 per cent of the GNP and around 2 per cent of the total budget is all that the higher and technical education receives.

Table 6.4 : Public Expenditure on Higher and Technical Education in India as Percentage of GNP and Budget

Year	*As per cent of GNP*	*As per cent of Budget*
1990-91	0.61	2.09
1991-92	0.56	1.91
1992-93	0.55	1.90
1993-94	0.40	1.89
1994-95	0.39	1.87
1995-96	0.37	1.80
1996-97	0.35	1.74
1997-98	0.35	1.75
1998-99	0.39	1.86
1999-00	0.47	2.09
2000-01	0.49	2.29
2001-02	0.39	1.72
2002-03	0.40	1.72
2003-04 RE	0.37	1.63
2004-05 BE	0.34	1.60

Source: MHRD, Government of India, Analysis of Budgeted Expenditure (various years).

However, the expenditure incurred by the state governments in India shows a greater percentage share of both the total budget as well as their Gross State Domestic Product (GSDP). This is because

Table 6.5: Educational Expenditure as Percentage of Total Budgetary Expenditure and GSDP

State	Year	As per cent of Budgetary Expenditure	As per cent of GSDP
1. Andhra Pradesh	2006-07	18.03	3.03
2. Arunachal Pradesh	2005-06	12.55	7.01
3. Assam	2006-07	22.02	5.64
4. Bihar	2006-07	22.87	5.70
5. Chhattisgarh	2005-06	22.36	3.21
6. Goa	2005-06	15.97	2.82
7. Gujarat	2005-06	18.71	2.20
8. Haryana	2006-07	15.67	2.05
9. Himachal Pradesh	2006-07	19.53	4.83
10. Jammu and Kashmir	2004-05	9.05	3.20
11. Jharkhand	2006-07	21.16	3.41
12. Karnataka	2005-06	19.02	3.12
13. Kerala	2006-07	22.47	4.21
14. Madhya Pradesh	2006-07	18.78	3.38
15. Maharashtra	2005-06	24.27	2.93
16. Manipur	2006-07	16.92	5.82
17. Meghalaya	2006-07	16.93	5.08
18. Mizoram	2006-07	10.07	9.78
19. Nagaland	2004-05	13.92	4.39
20. Orissa	2006-07	16.75	3.11
21. Punjab	2006-07	12.45	2.23
22. Rajasthan	2006-07	20.02	3.57
23. Sikkim	2006-07	10.84	7.01
24. Tamil Nadu	2006-07	19.48	3.22
25. Tripura	2005-06	19.47	5.10
27. Uttarakhand	2006-07	21.97	4.77
26. Uttar Pradesh	2006-07	20.76	3.76
28. West Bengal	2005-06	18.52	2.44
29. A & N Islands	2005-06	8.21	7.64
30. Chandigarh	2005-06	21.28	2.35
31. Delhi	2005-06	25.46	1.57
32. Pondicherry	2006-07	16.07	5.14
ALL INDIA	2007-08	13.46	3.67 (% GDP)

Source: Analysis of Budgeted Expenditure on Education, GOI, MHRD, 2008

of the fact that, education, in spite of being a subject in 'concurrent list' now, is mainly financed by the state governments in India. The financing of higher education among the states in India differs widely. This is depicted in Table 6.5. Delhi is seen to spend the highest percentage of its budget, i.e. 25.46 per cent to education, followed by Maharashtra, Assam, Bihar, Chhattisgarh and Kerala devoting

24.27 per cent, 22.02 per cent, 22.87 per cent, 22.36 per cent and 22.47 per cent, respectively. The lowest share of budget at only 8.21 per cent is devoted to education by Andaman and Nicober Islands in 2005-06, while the national average in 2007-08 was 13.46 per cent of the budget. Thus, the major states devoted a larger share of their budgets to education and *vice-versa*. Public expenditure as percentage of GSDP is higher in North-Eastern states compared to the other parts of the country. Among all the states of India, Mizoram devoted the highest share, i.e. 9.78 per cent of its GSDP to education sector in 2006-07. Against the national average of 3.67 per cent (of GDP) in 2007-08, Delhi spent the lowest proportion at only 1.57 per cent of its GSDP in 2005-06.

Factually speaking, states in India are hesitant in mobilizing additional resources from within the states and, therefore, the dependence is largely on central assistance or their share in divisible central taxes. Thus, because of the financial crunch at the state level, public money to finance higher education is not coming up in required amount. However, owing to relative decline in the contribution from fees and donations, the contribution of the state funds is relatively very high.

Financing of Education in Mizoram

Fund for education in Mizoram mainly comes from the state government. So, a brief account of the grant-in-aid procedure with regard to school education and college level education, followed by an analysis of the various sources of finance for higher education in Mizoram is presented in the following section.

Grant-in-Aid Procedure in Mizoram

The genesis of the system of grants to educational institutions can be traced back to Wood's Despatch of 1854, which outlined Government of India's policy towards financing of education. The two main objectives of the colonial government in this regard were:

(i) Gradual withdrawal of the Government from the educational field; and

(ii) Encouragement of private enterprise through a system of grants-in-aid.

However, the first ever grant-in-aid to the universities was sanctioned much later. In 1905 the Government sanctioned ₹ 25 lakhs for universities and colleges, to be given at the rate of ₹ 5 lakhs per year. By 1918-19, the quantum of grants was raised to ₹ 43 lakhs. Subsequently upward revisions took place, the policy remaining unchanged (Azad, 1989). With the coming up of a national Government after Independence, the existing policies and procedures of grants-in-aid to institutions of higher education were modified. Thus, the Central and State Governments have emerged as the main source of financing of educational programmes, in general, and higher education, in particular.

In Mizoram, educational institutions recognized by the state government but managed by the private agencies are given grants-in-aid according to certain rules. For this purpose there are two patterns and procedures of grant-in-aid system in Mizoram – one governing the school education and other relating to college education. The Mizoram Aided School (Recurring and Non-recurring Grants-in-aid) Rules, 1990 govern the pattern and procedure of grant-in-aid under the school education, while the Mizoram College (Recurring and Non-recurring Grants-in-aid) Rules, 1990 govern the system for the college education. These two Rules replaced the earlier two rules: Recurring Grants-in-aid for General Maintenance Rules, 1975 and the Non-recurring Grants-in-aid Rules, 1976.

Procedure Relating to School Education

As per the Mizoram Aided School (Recurring and Non-recurring Grants-in-aid) Rules, 1990 the approved expenditure of a school comprises the salaries of the teacher and other staff appointed with the approval of the Director or any other officer authorized by him in his behalf to the extent and according to the scales of pay as prescribed by the Government from time to time. The state government is the competent authority to sanction grants under these rules.

The non-recurring grants-in-aid are of the following categories:

(i) Grants for the construction/renovation of building involving major addition and repairs; and
(ii) Other admissible non-recurring grants include the construction of classroom and laboratory as well as for the strengthening of library facilities; for organization of sports and other competitions; and for conducting tours for students and teachers.

The Grants-in-aid Rules classified recognized schools into two groups: (i) Government aided schools which receive recurring and non-recurring grants-in-aid for general maintenance under the grants-in-aid system, and (ii) Unaided recognized schools which are private schools run by non-government organizations and they do not receive any grants-in-aid from the government.

The sanctions made by the government to the schools under the provisions of the said Rules are subject to audit by the authorized audit officers of the Accountant General and the examiner of the state/local accounts.

Procedure Relating to College Education

'Deficit Grants-in-aid' and 'Ad-hoc Grants-in-aid' are the two categories of recurring grants-in-aid for general maintenance of colleges in Mizoram.

The grants-in-aid are governed, among others by the following conditions:

(i) The institution shall not have under its employment any unqualified staff;
(ii) It shall have a minimum enrolment of 60 in case of College with only Pre-University classes and 150 in case of degree colleges with proper affiliation from the affiliating University; and
(iii) It must have been in existence for a minimum period of three years running effectively on its own resources and/any ad-hoc grant received from the government.

The approved income of a college includes the total income derived from tuition fees, fines, subscription, endowments and grant from local bodies or authorized but does not include any grants paid from the state fund. Other approved income consists of voluntary contributions or donations collected and voluntary contributions by the parents or guardians for the construction of any building for the college or its hostel.

The approved expenditure of college comprises the salaries of the teachers and staff appointed with the approval of the Director or any other officer authorized by him on his behalf to the extent and according to the scales of pay prescribed by the government from time to time. The government is the competent authority to sanction any grant under this Rule.

The Rules also stipulated that the college should have a Reserve Fund of ₹ 35,000.00 in respect of college with Pre-University courses only and ₹ 50,000.00 in respect of college with degree courses.

The non-recurring grants-in-aid are of the following categories:

(a) Grants for construction/renovation involving major addition and repair entailing heavy expenditure and/purchase of institution building including hostel building and staff quarters, play fields, fencing, etc.
(b) Other admissible non-recurring grants consist of the construction of classrooms, common rooms, laboratory, hostel, furniture; purchase of library books; for organization of sports and other competition; for conducting educational tours and excursions; organization of seminar, etc.

Sources of Finance for Higher Education in Mizoram

The various sources of finance for higher education in Mizoram are presented in Table 6.6. A glance over the table reflects the same trend that we find at the national level (Table 6.2). While the public sources of finance shows an upward trend, the private sources represent a downward trend, except for the years 1976-77 and 1980-81.

From the analysis of Table 6.6 some important points may be outlined as under:

(i) The share of State Government in financing higher education remained to be the highest during the period under

Table 6.6: Sources of Finance for Higher Education in Mizoram

(Amount in ₹Lakhs)

Year	*State Govt.*	*Local Bodies UGC*	*Fees*	*Endowments and others*	*Total*
1976-77*	25.5	2.0	3.6	0.4	31.5
	(80.9)	(6.3)	(11.4)	(1.3)	(100)
1980-81*	60.6	4.3	9.2	4.2	78.2
	(77.3)	(5.5)	(11.8)	(5.4)	(100)
1990-91	456.2	25.8	34.8	14.7	531.5
	(85.8)	(4.9)	(6.5)	(2.8)	(100)
2000-01	2158.1	82.6	163.4	53.7	2457.8
	(87.8)	(3.4)	(6.6)	(2.2)	(100)
2007-08	4357.3	264.2	328.7	92.5	5042.7
	(86.4)	(5.2)	(6.5)	(1.8)	(100)

Note: Figures in the parentheses show percentage to total.

Source: 1. * Directorate of School Education, Government of Mizoram, Aizawl.

2. State Budgets and Directorate of Higher and Technical Education, Mizoram.

consideration. It was recorded at 80.9 per cent of the total in 1976-77 and had increased to 86.4 per cent in 2007-08. The lowest amount contributed was 77.3 per cent in 1980-81. In absolute terms, the amount contributed by the State Government had increased 171 times during the said period.

(ii) The share of UGC and other government bodies have, throughout the period under consideration, been very low, being only 6.3 per cent at the highest in 1976-77. The amount contributed was 3.4 per cent in 2000-01, which was the lowest. The percentage contributions of this source were slightly higher at 4.9 per cent, 5.2 per cent and 5.5 per cent in 1990-91, 2007-08 and 1980-81, respectively.

(iii) The relative share of fee also has undergone considerable changes. However, fee remained as the second most important source of finance for higher education in Mizoram. In 1976-77 and 1980-81 fee contributions were 11.4 per cent and 11.8 per cent, respectively. The share came down to 6.6 per cent in 2000-01 and remained constant at 6.5 per cent in 1990-91 and 2007-08.

(iv) Endowments and others contributed the least share of finance for higher education in Mizoram. It contributed the highest share at 5.4 per cent of the total fund in 1980-81. The percentage share, then, fell down to 2.8 in 1990-91. It had further declined to 2.2 per cent in 2000-01 and 1.8 per cent in 2007-08. The lowest contribution was recorded at only 0.4 per cent in 1976-77.

The relative contribution of private *versus* public sources of fund for higher education reversed by 1980-81, with the contribution of public sources declining from 87.3 per cent of the total in 1976-77 to 83 per cent in 1980-81, and that of private sources increasing from 12.7 to 17 per cent during the same period. Contribution of public sources then increased to 90.7 per cent in 1990-91 and subsequently to 91.2 and 91.6 per cent in 2000-01 and 2007-08, respectively. On the other hand, the contribution of private sources declined to 9.3 per cent in 1990-91 and further to 8.8 per cent in 2000-01 and finally to 8.4 per cent in 2007-08. These trends are shown in Table 6.7. In this table public sources include contribution of the state government, local bodies and UGC. Private sources include fees, endowments and others.

Table 6.7: Public and Private Sources of Finance to Higher Education in Mizoram

(*Amount in ₹ Lakhs*)

Year	Public Sources	Index	Private Sources	Index	Total	Index
1976-77	27.5 (87.3)	100	4.0 (12.7)	100	31.5 (100)	100
1980-81	64.9 (83)	236	13.4 (17)	335	78.2 (100)	248
1990-91	482.0 (90.7)	1754	49.5 (9.3)	1238	531.5 (100)	1685
2000-01	2240.7 (91.2)	8155	217.1 (8.8)	5428	2457.8 (100)	7791
2007-08	4621.5 (91.6)	16822	421.2 (8.4)	10530	5042.7 (100)	15985

Note: Figures in brackets indicate percentages.

Source: Derived from Table 6.6.

Table 6.7 shows that while a reversal has taken place in the relative contribution of private and public sources of finance, the index showing increase in the contribution of different sources shows:

(i) One hundred and sixty times increase in the finance for higher education.
(ii) Contribution of public sources increased by 168 times.
(iii) Contribution of private sources increased by 105 times.

These trends reflect government's policy in making higher education accessible to students belonging to the weaker sections of society. The relative contribution of private sources (both fees and endowments etc.) having fallen considerably, greater burden is falling on the exchequer of the State Government, thus making educational finance in Mizoram more public finance oriented.

Government Source

In spite of the fact that, the amount of government expenditure increased by 168 times in nominal terms, it increased by nearly 20 times in real terms, during the period 1976-77 to 2007-08 (Table 6.8). At constant prices the contribution of government rose continuously from ₹ 108.7 lakhs to ₹ 2142.6 lakhs during the said period.

Table 6.8: Contribution of Government Sources to Higher Education in Mizoram

(In ₹ Lakhs)

Year	Total amount at Current Prices	Total Amount at Constant Prices (1993-94 = 100)	Index of Column 2	Index of Column 3	Share in Total Educational Finance (100%)
1	2	3	4	5	6
1976-77	27.5	108.7	100	100	87.3
1980-81	64.9	175.9	236	162	83.0
1990-91	482.0	654.0	1754	602	90.7
2000-01	2240.7	1439.1	8156	1324	91.2
2007-08	4621.5	2142.6	16822	1971	91.6

Source: Computed on the basis of data given in Table 6.6.

During the period 1980-81 and 1990-91, the quantitative expansion of higher education was the highest in the state. Consequently, the government contribution also hiked 6 times in 1990-91 as compared to the year 1976-77 (column 5 of the above Table 6.8). It increased further by 13 and 20 times in 2000-01 and 2007-08, respectively.

The most important source of finance for institutions of higher education is the government itself which provides financial assistance primarily through grants.

Grants may be (a) federal government grants or (b) state government grants. State grants are more important for State Universities and Colleges. For the Central Universities federal grants only constitute government sources. Federal grants both to the State as well as Central universities are routed through the University Grants Commission (UGC). Thus, the State Government and the UGC are the two important sources of revenue for the State universities and colleges. State grants may be classified into:

(i) Maintenance or block grants for day to day functioning;
(ii) Development grants which are given by the government to universities on a matching basis to UGC grants; and
(iii) Non-recurring grants for building, equipment etc.

The system of grants, though an essential element in financing of higher education, is far from satisfactory. Both federal and state grants are characterized by a high degree of complexity which many a times results in non-utilization and lapsing out of the grants (Tilak, 1998). Other shortcomings of grants are:

(i) State grants are generally inadequate. The amount of grants provided is not sufficient enough to fulfil the financial requirements of the institutions of higher education. Universities and colleges are perpetually in financial difficulties.
(ii) In disbursing grants to the institutions, the government does not show much consideration for equality, which results in glaring inter-institution disparities.
(iii) While releasing grants, the government does not stick to any

time schedule that would suit the needs of the institutions receiving it. Grants are often released at the fag-end of the financial year while need for grants is felt much earlier and the institutions find it difficult to meet their financial requirements and have to resort to overdraft from banks which increases their financial burden. Thus, uncertainties regarding actual amount of grant that would be obtained as well as delay in the release of grants adds to the financial pressures of the higher educational institutions.

(iv) In the case of federal grants which are given for developmental needs of universities, the UGC provides for capital requirements like buildings and equipments, its maintenance being the responsibility of the university, either from the State grants or from its own resources. This is also true of development grants, which are given on a matching basis. It is often difficult for the State governments to meet these financial obligations with the result that full potential of assistance from the UGC cannot be realized.

(v) While giving financial assistance, the UGC does not care to level down inter-university or inter-state inequalities. In the case of Central Universities, for instance, 90 per cent or more of their financial requirements come from the UGC, while it accounts for barely 5 per cent of the income of the State Universities (Azad, 1975).

(vi) The UGC provides development or Plan grants only. Once the Plan is over, it becomes the responsibility of the respective State Government to continue the development schemes, which is not always able to do on account of financial constraints. Thus, lack of coordination between the State Governments and the University Grants Commission, and the grant policies of the latter are not conducive to the development of higher educational institutions.

Internal Sources

(A) Fee: The second most important source of finance for higher education is fees, although its share in total finance has been falling over the years. An analysis of the contribution of fees is provided in Table 6.9.

Table 6.9: Contribution of Fee to Higher Education in Mizoram

(In ₹ Lakhs)

Year	Total amount at Current Prices	Total Amount at Constant Prices (1993-94=100)	Index of Column 2	Index of Column 3	Share in Total Educational Finance (100%)
1	2	3	4	5	6
1976-77	3.6	14.2	100	100	11.4
1980-81	9.2	24.9	256	175	11.8
1990-91	34.8	47.2	967	332	6.5
2000-01	163.4	104.9	4539	738	6.6
2007-08	328.7	152.4	9131	1073	6.5

Source: Computed on the basis of data given in Table 6.6.

It is seen from Table 6.9 that, while at current prices the contribution of fees has gone up from ₹ 3.6 lakhs in 1976-77 to ₹ 328.7 lakhs in 2007-08, at constant prices it has increased from ₹ 14.2 lakhs to ₹ 152.4 lakhs over the same period. A glance over the indices of growth (columns 4 and 5) shows that while total contribution of fees at current prices increased by 91 fold, it grew only 14 times at constant prices.

As the demand for higher education is ever-expanding the quantum of public funding is also increasing considerably, thereby befalling the State Government under severe financial strain. At the same time, the share of fee to total finance has been falling (column 6). Thus, there arises the need to adopt a more rational fee structure. The people have become accustomed to a highly subsidized higher education system. It is also true that the large majority of the people cannot afford more than what they are already paying. (Apart from fees, individuals also have to spend on books, stationery, conveyance etc.). In this situation a discriminatory fee structure based on cost of education, household income level etc., may be appropriate. Thus, the selective and not general fee rise would not fall heavily on the people while at the same time more resources could be mobilized.

(B) Endowments and Others: Generally, endowments and donations are given for some specific purpose like construction of hostels, library, laboratory or classrooms. The donors may be individuals – alumni or businessmen and industrialists as well as

philanthropic or business organizations. In the total finance for higher education the share of endowments etc., is the least. Table 6.10 shows the contribution from 'endowment and other' category.

Table 6.10 : Contribution of Endowment and other Sources to Higher Education in Mizoram

(In ₹ Lakhs)

Year	*Total amount at Current Prices*	*Total Amount at Constant Prices (1993-94=100)*	*Index of Column 2*	*Index of Column 3*	*Share in Total Educational Finance (100%)*
1	2	3	4	5	6
1976-77	0.4	1.6	100	100	1.3
1980-81	4.2	11.4	1050	713	5.4
1990-91	14.7	19.9	3675	1244	2.8
2000-01	53.7	34.5	13425	2156	2.2
2007-08	92.5	42.9	23125	2681	1.8

Source: Computed on the basis of data given in Table 6.6.

Although the amount of income from this source went on increasing continuously both in current and constant prices over the period under consideration, the relative share to the total finance was rather declining since 1980-81. At current prices the income from endowments and others was only ₹ 0.4 lakhs, which by four years time increased to ₹ 4.2 lakhs in 1980-81. By the next two decades, i.e. in 1990-91 and 2000-01 the amount rose to ₹ 14.7 lakhs and ₹ 53.7 lakhs, respectively. Finally, by the year 2007-08 the contribution of this source was ₹ 92.5 lakhs only. The index of growth (column 4) shows that the contribution of endowments and others increased 231 times during the entire period under consideration. However, in real terms the amount increased from ₹ 1.6 lakhs in 1976-77 to ₹ 42.9 lakhs in 2007-08, registering a 27 fold increase (column 4) during the said period.

The relative contribution of this source to the total educational finance increased to 5.4 per cent in 1980-81 from a mere 1.3 per cent in 1976-77. This is the highest relative share during the entire period under study. After that, the share sharply came down to 2.8 per cent in 1990-91, and then marginally declined to 2.2 per cent in 2000-01 and finally to 1.8 per cent in 2007-08.

In 1976-77 the amount of donations, endowments and others at constant prices was ₹ 1.6 lakhs when there were only 6 institutions of higher education in Mizoram. As the number of institutions increased to 12 the income from this source also increased to ₹ 11.4 lakhs by the year 1980-81. The same trend is observed in the next decade, i.e. between 1980-81 and 1990-91 when the institutions further increased to 21 and the amount of endowment contribution stood at ₹ 19.9 lakhs. After that, the amount rose to ₹ 34.5 lakhs in 2000-01 and ₹ 42.9 lakhs in 2007-08, when the number of institutions were 25.

It appears from the above analysis that endowments have lagged too far behind in their contribution to educational finance. This could be either due to the apathy of the people towards the educational system or may be on account of claims of other sectors on the contributions made by the philanthropists and their organizations. At the other end, unprecedented growth of the higher education sector in terms of student enrolment, number of institutions, diversified courses, and escalation in costs has all contributed to the increasing financial requirements of this sector. So, considering the contribution of endowments in the 1980s and early 90s it seems an important alternative to explore the potential of this source for raising more resources, in spite of the fact that these are only voluntary contributions and the deserving institutions have no control over them.

REFERENCES

Azad, J.L. (1975), *Financing of Higher Education in India*, Sterling Publishers, New Delhi.

Azad, J.L. (1989), "State Grants: Patterns, Procedures and Policies" in *Higher Education in India – The Institutional Context* (ed.) Amrik Singh, G.D. Sharma, Konark Publishers, Delhi.

CABE (2005): 'Financing of Higher and Technical Education', report of the CABE Committee, NIEPA, New Delhi.

Carnoy, M. (1999), *Globalisation and Educational Reform: What Planners Need to Know*, Report No.63, International Institute of Educational Planning, Paris.

Government of India (1998-99) 'Economic survey'.

Government of India, MHRD, Analysis of Budgeted Expenditure (various years).

Government of India (1995), MHRD, *Educational Expenditure in India*, New Delhi.

Government of Mizoram, Directorate of Higher and Technical Education, Mizoram.

Government of Mizoram, Directorate of School Education, Aizawl.

Government of Mizoram, Finance Department, State Budgets (various years).

Government of Mizoram, Planning and Programme Implementation Department.

Ilon, L. (1994), "Structural Adjustment and Education; Adapting to a Growing Global Market", *International Journal of Educational Development*, Vol. 14, No. 2.

Reddy, G. Ram, (1995) "Financing of Higher Education in India" in *Perspectives in Education*, Vol. II, No.1.

Stewart, F. (1996), "Globalisation and Education", *International Journal of Educational Development*, Vol.16, No.2.

Tilak, J.B.G. (1988), *University Finances in India*, Kluwer Academic Publishers, The Netherlands.

Tilak, J.B.G. (2001), "Education and Globalisation: The Changing Concerns in Economics of Indian Education, Editorial", *Perspectives in Education*, Vol.17, Special Issue.

UNESCO-UIS/OECD (2005) 'Education Trends in Perspective-Analysis of the World Education Indicators'.

7

Major Findings and Conclusion

Introduction

Although education in Mizoram is of about a century now, the state has achieved remarkable progress in this field, occupying the status of the second literate state in India today. Formal education was founded in Mizoram only with the arrival of the two Christian missionaries. Their first important contribution for the people of Mizoram was preparation of Alphabets based on Roman scripts. The first primary school was started at Aizawl in 1898 and in rural areas in 1901. The first Upper Primary School was started in 1907 and the first High School came up in 1944. In 1903 the government started giving grants-in-aid to schools maintained by the missionaries and also provided other incentives to the students, which marked the beginning of a new era in the expansion of education. Higher education in the state started quite late with the establishment of the first college in 1958. The present piece of work has made an attempt to analyze the public and private cost of higher education in Mizoram on the basis of data collected from a field survey of the higher educational institutions in the state and the students studying therein. Besides this, data were also collected from several published as well as unpublished records of the government departments and other relevant secondary sources. The main outcomes of the in-depth analysis in the foregoing chapters are abridged as major findings in the following section.

Major Findings

- The study finds that the literacy rate in Mizoram had increased from 36.23 per cent in 1951 to 88.80 per cent in 2001, while at the national level the literacy rate rose from 18.33 to 65.38 per cent during the same period. The study also reveals that, female literacy rate in Mizoram was higher than the national average as well as the all-India female literacy rate as per 1961 Census. In the subsequent censuses of 1971, 1981, 1991 and 2001 the female literacy rate of Mizoram exceeded the national average as well as male and female literacy rates.
- District-wise literacy rate shows that Aizawl district tops the rate at 96.50 per cent, while Lawngtlai district records the least at 64.70 per cent. Out of the eight districts of Mizoram four districts are seen to have literacy rate lower than the state-average of 88.80 per cent and another four districts above it.
- As regards enrolment the study finds that, the total number of students enrolled in various levels of education increased from 205321 in 2000-01 to 285499 in 2008-09, registering a growth rate of 3.37 per cent per annum. The highest growth rate of enrolment among all levels of education in the state is observed at 15.88 per cent per annum in the case of post graduate level, while the least is (–)1.63 per cent per year in case of professional education. As for the percentage share of enrolment, primary level accounts for 50.30 to 53.20 per cent of the total during the said period which is the highest, while enrolment in professional colleges accounts for the least. Out of the total enrolment, professional colleges constituted only 0.26 per cent in 2000-01, which has just halved to 0.13 per cent in 2008-09.
- The study reveals that, at primary level the number of teachers increased at an annual growth rate of 7.49 per cent, which is higher than the growth rate of schools at 4.49 per cent. However, in case of middle, high and higher secondary schools the number of teachers grew at a lower rate than that of the institutions. As for higher education, except in case of

university, the number of teachers showed a declining trend over the period under consideration. However, the number of institutions declined in case of general and professional education, while it remained constant in case of polytechnics and university.

- The study finds that, except for technical education, Aizawl district is seen to comprise the highest number of educational facilities in all respects and at all levels. Further, as the stages of education increase less and less decentralization of educational infrastructure in the state is observed.
- In spite of the fact that professional and vocational education in Mizoram encompasses the areas like paramedical, agro-forestry, law, teachers training, engineering and technology, management and computer education, the facilities and levels are mostly inadequate. This is due to the recent establishment of most of the institutions and diversification of courses. The open and distance education gathered momentum only with the establishment of IGNOU Regional Centre, Aizawl in December 2000, although the ODL system was there in the state for the last two decades.
- The study examined the trend of budgetary expenditure on education for the period 1997-98 to 2009-10. It was found that budgetary expenditure on education has been continually increasing, except the reversals in 2003-04 and 2004-05, during the period under consideration. In nominal terms it increased 4.7 times over the period, i.e. from ₹ 9561.85 lakhs in 1997-98 to ₹ 44589.55 lakhs in 2009-10. This shows an annual growth rate of 11.81 per cent. However, in real terms the expenditure on education rose only 2.5 times, increasing at the rate of 6.37 per cent per annum during the said period.
- While expenditure on school education increased from ₹ 8531.85 lakhs to ₹ 37993.19 lakhs registering a growth rate of 11.51 per cent per year, the amount incurred on higher education rose from ₹ 1030.00 lakhs to ₹ 6596.36 lakhs, showing an annual compound growth rate of 14.05 per cent during the period under consideration. At constant prices, the annual growth rates of public expenditure on school education and higher education were 6.08 and 8.49 per cent, respectively.

- Another important finding of the study is that, the ratio of higher educational expenditure to total educational expenditure was at its lowest level of 10.39 per cent in 1999-2000 and it touched its highest level in 2001-02 with the figure reading at 17.56 per cent. Except for the year 2001-02, for all the years between 1997-98 and 2009-10, the ratio of higher educational expenditure to total budgetary expenditure remained between the range of 1.15 and 1.92 per cent. This shows the sheer negligence of the higher educational sector by the state government. Higher educational expenditure as a ratio of state's income (NSDP) was as low as 0.82 per cent in 1999-2000, which continually increased to 2.03 per cent in 2001-02. After that, it started declining and reached 1.48 per cent in 2006-07. Since then, the ratio continued to improve until it reached the highest figure at 2.65 per cent in 2009-10.
- During the 13-year period between 1997-98 and 2009-10, plan expenditure on higher education in Mizoram grew at a compound rate of 19.46 per cent, while non-plan expenditure went up by 10.03 per cent and total educational expenditure rose by 14.05 per cent per annum. Plan expenditure varied between 31.15 to 65.00 per cent and non-plan expenditure between 35.00 to 68.85 per cent during the same period. Thus, the share of non-plan expenditure on higher education in Mizoram constitutes a greater proportion of total educational expenditure.
- Regarding public expenditure on higher education the study shows that, at current prices it has gone up from ₹ 1010 lakhs in 1997-98 to ₹ 3759.74 lakhs in 2007-08, registering a growth rate of 13.45 per cent per annum. However, in real terms, i.e., at constant prices (1993-94=100), the compound annual growth rate was only 8.54 per cent.
- Another feature of public expenditure on higher education is that, the lion's share is incurred on recurring expenditure (85 to 92%) leaving only 8 to 15 per cent for non-recurring items. Thus, the negligible share of non-recurring expenditure means poor capital formation in education.

- During the period 1997-98 to 2007-08, recurring expenditure grew at an annual compound rate of 13.92 per cent and non-recurring expenditure by 10.24 per cent, at current prices. But the growth rates, when converted into constant prices, were 8.63 and 5.08 per cent, respectively.
- The study also reveals that the public cost of education incurred on general degree colleges has increased from ₹ 847.74 lakhs in 1997-98 to ₹ 3243.69 lakhs in 2007-08, recording a growth rate of 13.84 per cent per annum. The amount of expenditure increased from ₹ 76.02 lakhs to ₹ 198.40 lakhs and from ₹ 86.24 lakhs to ₹ 317.65 lakhs, resulting to an annual compound growth rate of 10.81 and 11.39 per cent, in case of professional colleges and technical institutions, respectively, during the same period.
- As to the per unit public cost of higher education in Mizoram the study finds that it has been continually on an increase during the study period, except the reversals in 2003-04 to 2005-06. At current prices, it grew from ₹ 13760.22 in 1997-98 to ₹ 58810.26 in 2007-08, registering an annual growth rate of 14.64 per cent. While, in real terms, the growth rate was 9.24 per cent per annum during the same period as the unit cost rose from ₹ 10361.61 to ₹ 27164.84.
- The growth rates of public expenditure per student were calculated to be 15.91, 12.85 and -4.58 per cent per annum in general degree colleges, professional colleges and technical institutions, respectively, between the period 1997-98 and 2007-08. In absolute terms, the figures have risen from ₹ 12836.77 to ₹ 59310.48 and from ₹ 12482.76 to ₹ 48272.51 in case of general degree colleges and professional colleges, respectively, and have declined from ₹ 67905.51 to ₹ 61920.08 in case of technical institutions during the same period. However, the growth rates in real terms were 10.45, 7.54 and -9.07 per cent per annum, respectively.
- The share of fee receipt to public cost per unit in Mizoram ranged from a low of 7.84 per cent to a high of 12.17 per cent during the period 1997-98 to 2007-08 with variations

from year to year. This low contribution of fee indicates to the high extent of subsidy in higher education (Table 5.23).

- The study finds that there is an inverse relationship between enrolment size and per unit public cost of higher education (Tables 5.24 and 5.25). On an average, a one unit increase in enrolment leads to a fall in public cost by nearly ₹ 9 per student in Mizoram. Similarly, in case of general degree colleges, professional colleges and technical institutions per unit public cost decreases by ₹ 13, ₹ 84 and ₹ 74, respectively, resulting from a one unit increase in enrolment.
- An attempt to estimate the optimum enrolment size resulted into both minimum and maximum number of students for different types of higher educational institutions. The optimum level of enrolment that minimizes unit cost in technical institutions was calculated to be 948 students. As for the whole State of Mizoram as well as for the general degree colleges and the professional colleges the level of enrolment that minimizes unit cost could not be estimated. However, the levels of enrolment that maximizes unit cost in Mizoram and the two types of colleges are given at 9503, 4298 and 600 students, respectively. Any deviation from these numbers will lead to a reduction in the unit cost.
- The study estimated the private cost of higher education in Mizoram for the academic year 2007-08 at ₹40819.95, with maximum amount being ₹ 1,10,300 and minimum amount being ₹ 24200.
- Further analysis of private cost finds that, expenditure on food (₹ 14,757.73) tops the items comprising 38 per cent of the total, followed by accommodation (₹ 11,430.43) which is 25.23 per cent, fees (₹ 5,801.32), i.e. 12.98 per cent, books and stationeries (₹ 5,103.18) accounting for 12.91 per cent, personal maintenance (₹ 4,940.91) constituting 12.82 per cent and conveyance (₹ 3,060.73) comprising 7.5 per cent.
- As to the socio-economic background, the study finds that 8.64 per cent students hail from families whose occupation is agriculture and allied activities, 16.82 per cent from self-employment, 21.36 per cent from business and 53.18 per cent from government service. Thus, it is crystal clear that

more than half of the students are the children of government servants, and pupils from agricultural families are lagging far behind in higher education.

- According to family income it is seen that 10.91 per cent students come from the income group of ₹ 0 - ₹ 1,00,000, 23.64 per cent from the income group of ₹ 1,00,000 - ₹ 1,50,00, 23.18 per cent from the income group of ₹ 1,50,000 - ₹ 2,00,000, 20.45 per cent from the income group of ₹ 2,00,000 - ₹ 2,50,000, 11.82 per cent from the income group of ₹ 2,50,000 - ₹ 3,00,000, 6.82 per cent from the income group of ₹ 3,00,000 - ₹ 3,50,000, and only 3.18 per cent are from the income group of ₹ 3,50,000 and above.
- Scholarship contribution to total private cost was calculated to be 8.10 per cent in the year 2007-08. The amount of scholarship received by a student does not even cover the admission fee paid by him (which is 10 per cent of the total private cost).
- The study estimated the total cost of higher education per student at ₹ 91,503.54 for the academic year 2007-08, which is the sum of net public cost (₹ 53,990.28) and net private cost (₹ 37,513.26) per unit. Net public cost and net private cost per unit were arrived at by deducting the transfer payments, viz., average fee from the former and scholarship per student from the latter. It is a clear finding of the study that, the net public cost is 1.44 times higher than the net private cost (Table 5.35).
- The present study identifies four different sources of finance (State Government, Local Bodies/UGC, Fees and Endowments and others) for higher education in Mizoram and finds that the State Government is the major contributor, while endowments contribute the lowest share.
- The share of State Government in financing higher education remained to be the highest during the period 1976-77 to 2007-08. It was recorded at 80.9 per cent of the total in 1976-77 and had increased to 86.4 per cent in 2007-08. The lowest amount contributed was 77.3 per cent in 1980-81. In absolute terms, the amount contributed by the State Government had increased 171 times during the said period.

- The share of UGC and other government bodies have, throughout the period under consideration, been very low, being only 6.3 per cent at the highest in 1976-77. The amount contributed was 3.4 per cent in 2000-01, which was the lowest. The percentage contributions of this source were slightly higher at 4.9 per cent, 5.2 and 5.5 per cent in 1990-91, 2007-08 and 1980-81, respectively.
- The relative share of fee also has undergone considerable changes. However, fee remained as the second most important source of finance for higher education in Mizoram. In 1976-77 and 1980-81, fee contributions were 11.4 and 11.8 per cent, respectively. The share came down to 6.6 per cent in 2000-01 and remained constant at 6.5 per cent in 1990-91 and 2007-08.
- Endowments and others contributed the least share of finance for higher education in Mizoram. It contributed the highest share at 5.4 per cent of the total fund in 1980-81. The percentage share, then, fell down to 2.8 in 1990-91. It had further declined to 2.2 per cent in 2000-01 and 1.8 per cent in 2007-08. The lowest contribution was recorded at only 0.4 per cent in 1976-77. The reasons for the low contribution of endowment to educational finance could be either due to the apathy of the people towards the educational system or may be on account of claims of other sectors on the contributions made by the philanthropists and their organizations.
- The relative contribution of private *versus* public sources of fund for higher education reversed by 1980-81, with the contribution of public sources declining from 87.3 per cent of the total in 1976-77 to 83 per cent in 1980-81, and that of private sources increasing from 12.7 to 17 per cent during the same period. Contribution of public sources then increased to 90.7 per cent in 1990-91 and subsequently to 91.2 and 91.6 per cent in 2000-01 and 2007-08, respectively. On the other hand, the contribution of private sources declined to 9.3 per cent in 1990-91 and further to 8.8 per cent in 2000-01 and finally to 8.4 per cent in 2007-08.

- The study also reveals that, the contribution of public sources increased by 168 times, while the contribution of private sources increased by 105 times during the period 1976-77 to 2007-08. These trends reflect government's policy in making higher education accessible to students belonging to the weaker sections of society. The relative contribution of private sources (both fees and endowments etc.) having fallen considerably, greater burden is falling on the exchequer of the State Government, thus making educational finance in Mizoram more public finance oriented.

Conclusion

Expenditure on education is considered as an important component of investment which brings direct and indirect benefit to an individual and to the society. In Mizoram it is seen that, the State Government spends only a negligible proportion of its budgetary resources on education, in general, and higher education, in particular. But the quantitative expansion of educational sector along with the qualitative improvement of the existing system requires that a huge amount of public resources be devoted to this crucial sector. At the same time, infrastructural development of the educational institutions should be strengthened by raising the quantum of non-recurring expenditure, which, in fact, amounts to capital formation in the educational sector and ensures better academic quality. The inverse relationship between enrolment and unit cost suggests that number of students be increased in the higher educational institutions, by means of amalgamation of less populous colleges or otherwise, in order to reduce cost per unit. Ways and means may be devised to mobilize more resources from the people, in general, and affluent parents, in particular, as public cost is higher than private cost in Mizoram and higher education is highly subsidized.

Bibliography

Agarwal, A.N. (1995): *Indian Economy: Problems of Development and Planning*, Wiley Eastern Limited, Delhi.

Agarwal, P.D. (1988): "Unit Cost in Conventional and Distance Education System," in B.K. Koul, *et al.*, (eds) *Studies in Distance Education*, AIU/IGNOU, New Delhi.

Agarwal, R.B. (1993): *Education – Financing of Higher Education in India,* Ganga Kaveri Publishing House. Varanasi.

Ahmad, Nighat (2002): *Economics of Higher Education in Uttar Pradesh*, Aligarh Muslim University Press, Aligarh.

Annual Plans, 1997-98 to 2007-08, Planning & Programme Implementation Department, Government of Mizoram, Aizawl.

Annual Report 2007-08, Mizoram University, Aizawl.

Ansari, N.M. (1988-89): "Financial Health of Universities: A Diagnostic Study". *Journal of Higher Education,* Monsoon-Spring, Vol. 1 l, Nos. 1-3. U.G.C., New Delhi.

Ansari, M.M. (1999): "Financial Support to Education by Industry An Assessment" Paper presented at National Seminar on Financing Education, National Institute of Educational Planning and Administration, New Delhi.

Ansari, M.M. (1990): *Education Industry Linkages, Association of Indian Universities.* New Delhi.

Arrow, K.J. (1973): "Higher Education as a Filter", *Jounal of Public Economics* 2 (3) July.

Arrow, K.J. (1993): "Excellence and Equity in Higher Education". *Education Economics,* Vol. 1, No.1.

Azad, J.L. (1975), *Financing of Higher Education in India*, Sterling Publications, New Delhi.

Azad, J.L. (1989), "State Grants: Patterns, Procedures and Policies" in *Higher Education in India – The Institutional Context* ed. Amrik Singh, G.D. Sharma, Konark Publishers, Delhi.

Azad, J.L. (1988): *Higher Education in India — The Deepening Financial Crisis,* Radiant Publishers. New Delhi.

Baldev, Mahajan, *et al.*, (1994): *Educational Administration in Mizoram* (Structures, Processes and Future Prospects), NIEPA, New Delhi.

Barro, R.J. and Lee, J.W. (1993): International Comparisons of Educational Attainment, *Journal of Monetary Economics*, 32, 3.

Becker, Gary S. (1975): *Human Capital : A Theoretical and Empirical Analysis (with Special Reference to Education)* 2nd Education, NBER, New York.

Bhanoji, Raom V.V. (1992): "A note on Financing Education: Towards a Strategy for the 1990s and Beyond". *Journal of Educational Planning and Administration.* Vol. VI. No. 1, January.

Blaug, M. and Woodhall, M. (1967): "Productivity Trends in British Secondary Education, 1950-63" In J. Hallak (ed) *Educational Costs and Productivity,* UNESCO, IIEP, Paris, (Mimeographed).

Blaug, M. (1970): *An Introduction into the Economics of Education* Penguin, London

Blaug, M. (1976): The Empirical Status of Human Capital Theory: A Slightly Jaundiced Survey, *Journal of Economic Literature* 14 (3), September.

Blaug, M. (1985): "Where Are We Now in Economics of Education?" *Economics of Education Review,* 4 (1).

Blaug, M. (1987): *The Economics of Education and the Education of an Economist,* Aldershot, Edward Elgar Pub.

Blaug, M. (ed.), (1992): *The Economic Value of Education,* Aldershot: Edward Elgar Pub.

Blaug, M. *et al.*, (1969): *Causes of Graduate Unemployment in India.* The Penguin Press, London.

Bottery, Mike (1992): *The Ethics of Educational Management,* London. Cassell.

Bottomly, J.A. (1972): *Studies in Institutional Management in Higher Education – University of Bradford; Cost and Potential Economics.* O.E.C.D. Paris.

Bowman, M.J. (1966): "The Human Investment Revolution in Economic Thought", *Ociology of Education* 39 (2).

Buchanan, James and Devletoglu, N.E. (1970): *Academia in anarchy: An Economic Diagnosis,* Basic Book Inc. Publishers. New York.

CABE (2005): 'Financing of Higher and Technical Education', report of the CABE Committee, NIEPA, New Delhi.

Carnoy, M. (1995): *International Encyclopedia of Economics of Education* Oxford, Pergamon.

Carnoy, M. (1999): "Globalisation and Educational Reform: What Planners Need to Know", Report No. 63, International Institute of Educational Planning, Paris.

Census of India (1981): Series – 31. Mizoram, Census of India, 1991. Series – 17. Mizoram and Census of India, 2001, Series – 16. Mizoram.

Chalam, K.S. (1986): *Finances Costs and Productivity of Higher Education.* Inter-India Publications, New Delhi.

Chaube, P.K. (1999): "Decentralization of Governance and Community Financing of Elementary Education", Paper presented at the National Seminar on Financing Education, NIEPA, New Delhi.

Colclough, C. (1996): "Education and the Market: Which Parts of the Neoliberal Solution are Correct?" *World Development.* Vol.24, No.4.

Coombs and Hallak, (1972): *Managing Educational Costs,* UNESCO: IIEP Oxford University Press, New York.

Datt, Rudder (1988): "Distance Education Versus Traditional Higher Education: A Cost Comparison," in B.N. Koul (eds) *Studies in Distance Education*, AIU/IGNOU, New Delhi.

Datt, Rudder (1969): "Unit costs of Education – A case study of Haryana Colleges" in H.N. Pandit (ed) *Measurement of Cost Productivity and Efficiency of Education*, NCERT, New Delhi.

Denison, E.F. (1962): "The Sources of Economic Growth in the United States and the Alternatives Before Us", Committee for Economic Development, New York.

Dey, B. (1969): "On Costing of Education," in H.N. Pandit (ed)

Measurement of Cost Productivity and Efficiency of Education, NCERT, New Delhi.

Garg, V.P. (1982): Cost Analysis of the University of Punjab, 1950-51 to 1974-75. *Indian Educational Review*, July.

Gautam, G.S. (1972): *Crisis in the Temples of Learning,* S. Chand and Company, New Delhi.

Government of India (1949): Report of the University Education Commission 1948-49 (Radha Krishnan Commission). Delhi.

Government of India (1966): Education and National Development — Report of the Education Commission 1964-1966 (Kothari Commission), New Delhi.

Government of India (1970): *Education and National Development* (Report of the Education Commission, 1964-66) NCERT, New Delhi.

Government of India (1986): *National Policy on Education.*

Government of India (1994): *Government Subsidies in India.* Discussion Paper. Ministry of Finance. Government of India. New Delhi.

Government of India (1995): *Educational Expenditure in India*, MHRD, New Delhi.

Government of India (1998-99): 'Economic survey'.

Government of India : Census of India, 1951-2001.

Government of India: Analysis of Budgeted Expenditure MHRD, (various years).

Government of India: Office of the Economic Adviser, Ministry of Commerce and Industry, New Delhi.

Government of Mizoram (2009): Education Reform Commission of Mizoram Report, Aizawl.

Government of Mizoram : Economic Survey, Mizoram, 2008-09 and 2009-10, Planning and Programme Implementation Department.

Government of Mizoram : Statistical Abstract of Mizoram, 2007 and 2009, Directorate of Economics and Statistics.

Government of Mizoram, Directorate of Higher and Technical Education, Mizoram.

Government of Mizoram, Directorate of School Education, Aizawl.

Government of Mizoram, Finance Department, State Budgets (various years).

Government of Mizoram: *Statistical Handbook of Mizoram*, various years.

Graham, J.W. (1987): "International Educational Expenditures" in George Psacharopoulos (ed) *Economics of Education Research and Studies*, Pergamon Press, Oxford.

Gupta, A. (2005): "International Trend in Higher Education and the Indian scenario", Centre for Studies in Higher Education, CSHE-11-05, available at http://repositories, cdlib.org/cshe

Hallak, J. (1969): *The Analysis of Educational Costs and Expenditure*. UNESCO: IIEP, Paris.

Hanushek, Eric A. (1995): "Interpreting Recent Research on Schooling in Developing Countries", *The World Bank Research Observer,* Vol. 10, No.2..

Haq, Mahboobul & Haq, Khadija. (1998): *Human Development in South Asia -1998,* The Human Development Centre, Karachi: Oxford University Press.

Hluna, J.V. (1992): *Education and Missioneries in Mizoram*, Spectrum Publication, Guwahati/Delhi. http://www.mizoram.nic/about/physiography.htm

Husain, I.Z. (1967): "Returns to Education in India: An Estimate" in *Education as Investment.* Ed. Baljit Singh. Meenakshi Prakashan. Meerut.

Ilon, L. (1994): "Structural Adjustment and Education; Adapting to a Growing Global Market", *International Journal of Educational Development*, Vol.14, No.2

India Today (2007): State of the States, Volume. XXXII, No. 38, 18-24 September.

Institute of Applied Manpower Research (1975) *Pattern of Expenditure and Per Student Cost in Indian Institute of Technology*, New Delhi.

Institute of Applied Manpower Research (IAMR) (1964): *Cost study 1964*. New Delhi.

International Institute for Educational Planning (IIEP) (1972): *Educational Cost Analysis in Action: Case Studies for Planner, Vols. II & III.* UNESCO: IIEP, Paris.

Johnstone, B. (1989): "International Comparisons of Student Financial Support". in M. Woodhall (ed.). *Financial Support for, Students:*

Grants, Loans as Graduate Tax? Kogan Page Institute of Education. University of London, London.

Kabra, K.N. and Chaube, P.K. (1998): "Higher Education: Is it a Merit Service?". *University News* (Special Number) Vol. 36, No. 24.

Kalam, A.P.J. (2005): President's Address to the Nation on the Eve of Independence Day, 2004, Published in *Yojana,* September.

Kapur, J.N. (1977): *Current Issues in World Higher Education.* S. Chand and Co. New Delhi.

Khemani, *et al.,* (2006): "Higher Education Sector in India: Opportunities and Reforms", Foundation for Democratic Reforms, Hyderabad.

Kremer, Michael R. (1995): "Research on Schooling: What we know and what we don't—A Comment on Hanushek", *The World Bank Research Observer,* Vol. 10. No. 2.

Kulkarni, G.B. (1969): "Cost of Education in Commerce Colleges of Bombay 1962-63 to 1966-67" in H.N. Pandit (ed) *Measurement of Cost Productivity and Efficiency of Education*, NCERT, New Delhi.

Kumar, G. (2003): "Resource association Regions—Quest for a Development Strategy – A Case Study of Mizoram" in *Modernisation of the Mizo Soceiety* (ed.), R.N. Prasad and A.K. Agarwal, Mittal Publications, New Delhi.

Lakdawala, D.T. and Shah, K.R. (1978): *Optimum Utilization of Educational Expenditure in Gujarat.* Sardar Patel Institute of Economic and Social Research. Ahmedabad..

Lalliani (1990): "An Analystical study of the Primary Education in Mizoram during the Post-Independence period", Unpublished Ph.D. Thesis; Department of Education, NEHU, Shillong.

Laskar, B.I. (2010): "*Industrialisation in Mizoram: Problems and Prospects*, New Central Book Agency (P) Ltd., Kolkata.

Lawma,T. (1986): "Earning – Occupation – Education Inter-Relations: A case study of North-East India", *Manpower Journal,* Vol. XXII, No. I, April-June.

Lawma, T. (1990): *Market Imperfections and Manpower Planning,* Commonwealth Publishers, New Delhi.

Levy, D.C. (1992): "Private Institutions of Higher Education". in B.C. Clark and G.R. Neave (Eds.) *Encyclcpedia of Higher Education,* Pergamon, Oxford.

Machlup, F. (1962): *The Production and Distribution of Knowledge in United States*, Princeton University Press, New Jersey.

Majumdar, Tapas. (1998): "Economics of Indian Education: The Emerging Policies". *Journal of Educational Planning and Administration,* Vol. XII. No. 1.

Manoharan, P.T. (1998.): Campus News. *University News.* Vol. 36, No. 14.

Manpower Profile (1998): India Year Book. Institute of Applied Manpower Research. New Delhi.

Mathew, E.T. (1991): *Financing Higher Education*, Concept Publishing Company, New Delhi.

Mathew, E.T. (1990): "Financing of Private Colleges in Kerala", *Economic and Political Weekly,* 28th April.

Maynard, J. (1971): *Some Micro-economics of Higher Education: Economies of Scale*, University of Nebraska, Lincoln, Nebraska.

McCall, A.G. (1977): *Lushai Chrysalis*, Tribal Research Institute, Aizawl.

Meier, Gerald M. (1995): *Leading Issues in Economic Development,* Oxford University Press. Delhi. 4th Ed.

Mingat, Alain and J.P. Tan (1985): "On Equity in Education again: An International Comparison", *Journal of Human Resources*, 20 Vol. No. 2 Spring.

Misra, A. (1967): *The Financing of Indian Education.* Asia Publishing House. Bombay.

Mizoram at a glance (2001): Directorate of Census Operations, Government of India. Aizawl, Mizoram.

Mukerji, K. and Krishnarao, N. (1967): Education and Economic Development in India between 1951 and 1961: An Empirical Investigation, in *Education as Investment.* Ed. Baljit Singh. Meenakshi Prakashan. Meerut.

Musgrave, R.A. (1966): *Financing of Education for Economic Growth,* O.E.C.D., Paris.

Muzammil Mohammad. (1995): "Flout the Rule and Pay the Price". *The Guardian.* London. Educational supplement, January 20.

Muzammil, Mohammad. (1989): *Financing of Education.* Ashish Publishing House. New Delhi.

Nagarjuna, B. & Narayana, D.L. (2005): *Economics of Human Resource Development: A Perspective Analysis*, Serials Publication, New Delhi.

Nanjundappa, D.M. (1994): *Finance and Management of Higher Education.* Deep and Deep Publications, New Delhi.

Nanjundappa, DM. (1976): *Working of University Finances*, Sterling Publishers. New Delhi.

Natarajan, S. (1990): *Introduction to Economics of Education*, Sterling Publications, New Delhi.

Natarajan, S. (1990): *Introduction to Economics of Education,* Sterling Publishers. New Delhi.

NIPFP (1977): *Government subsidies in India.* National Institute of Public Finance and Policy, New Delhi.

OECD (1995-97): *Education at a Glance : OECD Indicators,* Organisation for Economic Cooperation and Development, Paris.

OECD (1990): *Finance Higher Education: Current Patterns,* Organisation for Economic Cooperation and Development. Paris.

Organisation for Economic Co-operation and Development (OECD) (1977): *Educational Expenditure in France, Japan and the United Kingdom*, OECD, Paris.

Padmanabhan, C.B. (1967): "Education and Economic Growth : Progress and Problems", in *Education as Investment.* Ed. Baljit Singh, Meenakshi Prakashan, Meerut.

Panchamukhi, P.R. (1965): "Educational Capital in India", *Indian Economic Journal*, 12, Jan-March.

Panchmukhi, P.R. (1977): *Economics of University Finances : Basic Principles and Practice,* Dharwar: Centre for Multidisciplinary Research, Karnataka Historical Research Society, XVI.

Panchmukhi, P.R. (1987): "Trends in Financing of University Education", *Economics of Educational Finance: Studies in Economics of Educational Reform in India.* Himalaya Publishing House, Bombay, pp. 94-110.

Pandit, H.N. (1972): "Cost and Financing of Education—Private and Social Participation", *Indian Educational Review*, July, Vol 2, No. 2.

Patel, I.G. (July 1992): "Higher Education and Economic Development", *Journal of Educational Planning and Administration,.* Vol. VI. No. 3.

Prakash, S. (1977): *Educational System of India: An Econometric Study*, Concept Publishing Company, New Delhi.

Prakash, S. (1996): "Optimisation in Resource Use in Elementary

Education in India" in Koti, K.R. *et al.*, (ed.) *Studies in Indian Economy (Prof. P.R. Mathur Memorial volume)*, Himalaya Publishing House, Bombay.

Prakash, Shri and Chowdhury, Sumitra. (1994): *Expenditure on Education – Theory, Models and Growth*, NIEPA, New Delhi.

Psacharopoulos, G. (1972): *The Return to Education: An International Comparison,* Elsevier, Amsterdam.

Psacharopoulos, G. (1973): *Returns to Education,* Elsevier, New York.

Psacharopoulos, G. (1990): "Priorities in the Financing of Education". *International Journal of Educational Development,* Vol. 10. No.2-3.

Psacharopulos, G. and M. Woodhall. (1985): *Education and Development,* Oxford University Press and World Bank. New York.

Rao, V.K.R.V. (1966), *Socio-economic Survey of Greater Delhi City*, Asia Publishing House.

Raza, Moonis (Ed). (1991): *Higher Education in India Retrospect and Prospect.* Association of Indian Universities. New Delhi.

Reddy, D.N. and Kishore, K.L. (2009): "Revamping Higher Education: Need of the Hour", *University News*, 47 (45), November 9-15.

Reddy, G. Ram, (1995): "Financing of Higher Education in India" in *Perspectives in Education*, Vol. II, No.1.

Riddell, A.R. (1993): "The Evidence of Public/Private Educational Trade-offs in Developing Countries", *International Journal of Educational Development,* Vol. 13, No.4.

Robbins Committee. (1963): *Report of the Committee on Higher Education,* HMSO, London.

Robinson, E.A.G. and Vaizey, J.E. (Eds.). (1966): *The Economics of Education,* MacMillan, London. New York.

Rosanga, O. (1990): "Economic History of Mizoram (1900-1940)", (Unpublished Ph.D. Thesis), Department of History, Delhi University, Delhi.

Salim, A. Abdul (1993): "Private Cost of Higher Education in Kerala: Socio-Economic Analysis" *Journal of Higher Education*, Volume 16 No. 3 Summer.

Salim, A. Abdul (1996): "Institutional Cost of Higher Education – A Case Study of Kerala", *Manpower Journal,* Vol. XXXII. No. I, April-June.

Saraf, S.N. (1988): "Higher Education and Five Year Plans: Policies, Plans and Perspectives" in Singh and Sharma (Eds.), *Higher Education in India: The Social Context,* Konark. New Delhi.

Saxena, Pradeep Kumar. (1988-89): "Recent Enrolment Trends in Higher Education in India". *Journal of Higher Education,* Vol. 14. Nos. 1-3, U.G.C., New Delhi.

Schultz, T.W., (1960): "Capital Formation by Education", *Journal of Political Economy,* Vol. 68, December.

Schultz, T.W., (1961): "Education and Economic Growth" in H.G. Richey (ed) *Social Forces influencing American Education,* Chicago.

Schultz, T.W. (1961): "Investment in Human Capital", *American Economic Review*, 51 (1), March.

Schultz, T.W. (1963): *The Economic Value of Education.* Columbia University Press, New York.

Schultz, T.W. (1962): "Reflections on Investment in Man", *Journal of Political Economy,* September-October.

Shaffer, H.G. (1961): "Investment in Human Capital: Comment", *American Economic Review*, Vol. 52, No. 4.

Shah, K.R. (1969): "Expenditure on Professional School Education in India, 1950-51 to 1960-61" in H.N. Pandit (ed) *Measurement of Cost Productivity and Efficiency of Education,* NCERT, New Delhi.

Shah, K.R. (1969): "Private Costs of Elementary Education" in H.N. Pandit (ed) *Measurement of Cost Productivity and Efficiency of Education,*NCERT, New Delhi.

Shaikh, S. and Gawali, V. (2009): 'Does India Need Foreign Universities?' *University News*, 47 (39), September 28-October 4.

Sharma, G.D. (1980): *Institutional Costs of University Education – A Study of Costs and Efficiency of Indian University System,* AIU, New Delhi.

Sharma, G.D. and Mridula (1982): *Economics of College Education – A Study of Hindu College,* Delhi, AIU, New Delhi.

Sharma, M.M. (1992): *Financial Management of Universities in India,* Concept Publishing Company, New Delhi.

Sharma, Narayan Prasad (1993): *Economics of College Education: A Study of Non-Viable Colleges.* Anmol Publications, New Delhi.

Sharma, G.D. (1992): Higher Education: Resource or Policy Crunch", in *University News* Vol. XXX. No. 33.

Singh, A. and Sharma, G.D. (Eds.) (1981): *University and College Finances,* Association of Indian Universities. New Delhi.

Singh, Amrik and Sharma, G.D. (1988): *Higher Education in India The Social Context.* Konark Publishers, New Delhi.

Singh, Amrik and Sharma, G.D. (1989): *Higher Education in India: The Institutional Context,* Konark Publishers, New Delhi.

Singh, S. (2008): "Strategic Developmental Plan for Adoption of Information & Communication Technology (ICT) in College Libraries of Mizoram", (Unpublished Ph.D. Thesis), Department of Library and Information Sciences, Mizoram University, Aizawl.

Srinivasan, R. (1999): "Collegiate Education and Economic Growth in India", *University News,* Vo1.37, No.10.

Stewart, F. (1996): "Globalisation and Education", *International Journal of Educational Development*, Vol.16, No.2.

Strumillin, S.G. (1925): "Economic Significance of National Education", Reprinted in *The Economics of Education* (eds. Robinson, E.A.G., Vaizey, J.), London, Macmillan, 1966.

The Economic Times, New Delhi (1993): "Universities Struggle to Learn ABC of Finance". *Special Report*, 17th October, Sunday.

The International Encyclopaedia of Higher Education, (1977), Vol.5. Jossey-Bass Publishers. San Francisco.

Thobani, Mateen. (1983): *Charging User Fees for Social Services: The Case of Education in Malaw.* Staff Working Paper. No. 572. *World Bank.* Washington D.C.

Tilak, J.B.G. (1987): *The Economics of Inequality in Education,* Sage Publication India Pvt. Ltd., New Delhi.

Tilak, J.B.G. (1988): *University Finances in India*, Kluwer Academic Publishers, The Netherlands.

Tilak, J.B.G. (1993): "Financing Higher Education in India" in Sumas Chitnis & Phillip G. Altbach, (eds) *Higher Education Reform in India: Experience and Perspective*, Sage Publication Pvt. Ltd., New Delhi.

Tilak, J.B.G. (1993): "Unit Cost Analysis of Higher Education in India" in Devendra Thakur (ed)., *Education and Manpower Planning,* Deep & Deep Publication Pvt. Ltd., New Delhi.

Tilak, J.B.G. (1994): *Education for Development in Asia,* Sage Publication Pvt. Ltd., New Delhi.

Tilak, J.B.G. (2001): "Education and Globalisation: The Changing

Concerns in Economics of Indian Education, Editorial", *Perspectives in Education*,Vol.17, Special Issue.

Tilak, J.B.G. (2008): "Economics of Human Capital in India" in *Economics of Education and Health in India* (ed.) A.K. Thakur and Mbs. A. Salam, Deep and Deep Publications Pvt. Ltd., New Delhi.

Tilak, J.B.G. and V.N. Verghese (1983): "Resources for Education in India", *Occasional Paper*, No. 2, NIEPA, New Delhi.

Tilak, J.B.G. (1995): "On Pricing Higher Education", 2 *UGC Occasional Paper No.,* NIEPA, New Delhi.

Tilak, J.B.G. (1997a): "Lessons from Cost Recovery in Education". in C. Colclough (Ed.), *Marketising Education and Health in Developing Countries: Miracle or Mirage?,* Clarendon Press, Oxford.

Tilak, J.B.G. (1995b): "Higher Education at Cross Roads in India" in Buchert and K. King (Eds.) *Learning from Experience : Policy and Practice in Aid to Higher Education,* CESO Paperback, No.24. Centre for the Study of Education in Developing Countries, Hague.

Tilak, J.B.G. (1998): *NIEPA Occasional Paper: No. 26,* National Institute of Educational Planning and Administration. New Delhi.

Tilak, J.B.G. (1983b): "Analysis of Costs of Education". *Perspectives in Education,* Vol.5, No.4.

Tilak, J.B.G. (1991): "Privatisation of Higher Education", *Prospects : Quarterly Review of Education,* Vol.21, No.2.

Tilak, J.B.G. (1991): "International Trends in Costs and Financing of Higher Education: Some Tentative Comparisons between Developed and Developing Countries". *Higher Education Review,* Vol. 25. No.3, Summer.

Tilak, J.B.G. (1997b): "Effects of Adjustment on Education : A Review of Asian Experience". *Prospects,* Vol. 27, No.1.

UNDP: *Human Development in South Asia, 1998.* UNDP Office in Islamabad.

UNESCO (1997): *Statistical Year Book,* Paris (various years).

UNESCO-UIS/OECD (2005): "Education Trends in Perspective-Analysis of the World Education Indicators".

Vaizey, J. (1958): *Costs of Education,* Allen & Unwin, London.

Vaizey, J. and Sheehan, J. (1968): *Resources for Education. An Economic Study of Education in the United Kingdom,* 1920-1965, Allen & Unwin, London.

Vanlalchhawna (2006): *Higher Education in North East India*, Mittal Publications, New Delhi.

Weiler, H.N. (1984): "Aid for Education: The Political Economy of International Cooperation in Educational Development" in R.M. Garrett (Ed.), *Education and Development,* Croom Helm, London.

World Bank (1986): *Financing Education in Developing Countries: An Exploration of Policy Options,* Washington D.C.

World Bank (1995): *Higher Education: The Lessons of Experience, Development in Practice.* World Bank, Washington D.C.

Ziderman, Adrian and Douglas Albrecht (1995): *Financing Universities in Developing Countries,* Palmer Press. Washington D.C.

Zonunthara, S.R. (2001): "Working of Public Distribution System in Mizoram", (Unpublished Ph.D. Thesis), Department of Economics, NEHU, Shillong.

Index